Explorations in
Love and Sex

Books by Irving Singer

Explorations in Love and Sex

Sex: A Philosophical Primer

Feeling and Imagination: The Vibrant Flux of Our Existence

George Santayana, Literary Philosopher

Reality Transformed: Film as Meaning and Technique

Meaning in Life:
The Creation of Value
The Pursuit of Love
The Harmony of Nature and Spirit

The Nature of Love:
Plato to Luther
Courtly and Romantic
The Modern World

Mozart and Beethoven: The Concept of Love in their Operas

The Goals of Human Sexuality

Santayana's Aesthetics

Essays in Literary Criticism by George Santayana (editor)

The Nature and Pursuit of Love: The Philosophy of
Irving Singer (edited by David Goicoechea)

Explorations in
Love and Sex

Irving Singer

ROWMAN & LITTLEFIELD PUBLISHERS, INC.
Lanham • Boulder • New York • London

ROWMAN & LITTLEFIELD PUBLISHERS, INC.

Published in the United States of America
by Rowman & Littlefield Publishers, Inc.
4720 Boston Way, Lanham, Maryland 20706

12 Hid's Copse Road
Cumnor Hill, Oxford OX2 9JJ, England

British Cataloguing in Publication Information Available

Library of Congress Cataloging-in-Publication Data

Singer, Irving.
    Explorations in love and sex / Irving Singer.
        p.   cm.
    Includes bibliographical references and index.
    ISBN 0-7425-1238-X (alk. paper)
        1. Love. 2. Sex. I. Title.

 B945.S6573 E87 2001
 128'.46—dc21

                                        2001041704

Printed in the United States of America

∞™ The paper used in this publication meets the minimum
requirements of American National Standard for Information
Sciences—Permanence of Paper for Printed Library Materials,
ANSI/NISO Z.39.48–1992.

To David and Bronia

Contents

Preface

For as long as I can remember, I have always envied writers whose words seemed to leap upon the printed page without requiring prior or subsequent changes. Bertrand Russell says somewhere that he trained himself to complete his books in his mind before he picked up his pen and started addressing readers who might care about his thoughts. Another prolific author told me once that after his wife died he found that he could endure his unremitting grief only by writing something and then sending it immediately to the press. This then became habitual to him. My own experience as a writer has been very different, and totally unlike Russell's.

For me writing has always been an attempt to discover *through it* what I believe about some question that matters to me at a moment in my life. Composition is the means by which I search for insight about myself as a person who is able even to grapple with the important issues that I and others find challenging. I have never felt I have at hand a clearly formulated doctrine that is ready made before its communication, sanctioned perhaps by some godlike authority or by an inner light that allows me to see what no one else can.

My creative existence is therefore a series of explorations, none of them final or definitive and all of them a tentative preparation for later developments. My teaching and discussion with others, or my cogitation by myself, tend to be first drafts that I eventually reject as inadequate and in need of much revision. Only in consecutive writing and rewriting am I able to learn what I truly think about a problem that I confront at any time. The process of writing tells me what I should be writing about and what the world I know must be like in view of my ability to write about it at all.

I make these comments now in order to introduce the character of this book. It draws together philosophical explorations that have preoccupied me for many years. But it also extends these explorations in ways that I could not have foreseen previously. Some of the chapters have slumbered in a limbo of their own for decades simply because I felt unequal to the difficulties they occasioned. Only recently have I seen how I might reach a tentative solution of them, and only in the last few months have I been able to go through the many drafts that were needed to unravel the philosophical tangles inherent in them. Even the older of these chapters are new in the sense that they embody reasoning that has been changed or even redirected, in its specific content and sometimes in its general outlook. They have been altered to accommodate the current stages of my search for some degree of clarity.

There are two unifying strands that link the explorations to be encountered here. The first is the pluralism that underlies all my writing on the nature of love or sex or, for that matter, reality itself. The pluralistic orientation of my thinking is articulated most completely in *Feeling and*

Imagination: The Vibrant Flux of Our Existence.[1] While standing on their own, the chapters in the present effort can be read as an extension and refinement of that book's overall vision, though with particular emphasis upon the philosophy of love, sex, and compassion, and the writings of Kant, Schopenhauer, Bergson, and Ortega y Gasset among others.

As their second binding thread, several of these chapters are sequelae to material that appears in *Sex: A Philosophical Primer.*[2] That book says a little, but not very much, about ethical theory relevant to the nature of sex and sexual love. In this book I attempt further explorations into the morality of these responses, in themselves as well as in their relations to compassion, on the one hand, and what I call the sensuous and the passionate, on the other.

I am guided throughout by my belief that our inherited ideas about sex, love, and compassion have suffered from the common assumption that these three are in principle totally separate from each other. If we retain that shibboleth, it is hard to see how authentic sexual love can ever exist, or how compassion may be an element in either sex or love.

Presuppositions about the separability of sex, love, and compassion lie at the core of Kant's speculations in this area. I begin with him because his arguments are both penetrating and bizarre, though most of his contemporaries may well have found them obviously correct. For us he is a good point of departure since he distinguishes between an ethical type of love, concerned about the welfare of all human beings treated as autonomous persons, and another type (whose morality is always problematic) that results from "natural inclinations." Compassionate feelings, together with those that are sexual, he places in the second category. Like many others in the rationalist and theological traditions, Kant denies that the different kinds of responsiveness are inherently interrelated. It seems evident to him that, at best, they can have only external relations to each other. This assurance is foundational in his reflections about the possibility of one or another becoming morally justifiable.

Since Schopenhauer claims to detect inner relations between love and sex as well as love and compassion, he serves as a suitable contrast to Kant. But Schopenhauer interprets these phenomena in ways that seem radically mistaken to me. He reduces romantic love to libidinal sexuality, and he depicts the loving-kindness in compassion not only as the basis of morality but also as a sense of metaphysical fusion with all of life. In criticizing these notions, I provide a more thoroughly naturalistic portrait of the interpenetration among sex, love, and compassion. I nevertheless accept much of what Schopenhauer says about loving-kindness as a basis of morality.

In the writing that follows the first two chapters, I offer my latest, often considerably revised, ideas about the virtues and limitations of a pluralistic approach toward love and sex. In two panoramic chapters, originally given as television interviews, I trace the philosophy of love as it has developed from its beginnings in Ancient Greece up to the present. Earlier distinctions that I have made, for instance between appraisal and bestowal, are then amplified in replies to various critics or commentators and positioned within the context of what they consider interesting in my work. The chapters on Bergson and Ortega examine these modern masters in relation to themes that recur throughout my book. In the final pages I try to see whether a philosophical perspective such as mine can yield plausible suggestions about the affective life that people may experience in the twenty-first century.

Addressing this interwoven filament as I do, I find myself voyaging into strange and novel territory that some thinkers may want to colonize in the coming decades. My hope is that I can help them to create new methods and new concepts that will be useful for their own explorations. I am sure that the opportunities they may discover are enormous.

As with my other books, I am grateful for the assistance I have received from many persons: especially, in this case, from Herbert Engelhardt, Robert Fulford, David Goicoechea and the critics and commentators to whose writing I respond in chapter 6, Timothy J. Madigan, Ulrich Meyer, John Rundell, Josephine F. Singer, Alan Soble, and Robert C. Solomon.

I. S.

1

The Morality of Sex: Contra Kant

Philosophers who think that sex is just an instinctual and appetitive faculty oriented toward selfish gratification or reproductive need will always find its ethical status problematic. Under many circumstances, the satisfaction of both the instinct and the appetites related to it can be good or bad, right or wrong, ethically better or worse. Human sexuality is subject to this ambivalence of valuation in a way that does not apply to the sexuality of what are called "lower" species. We do not condemn these other animals because of the beastiality, or even cruelty, of their sexual responses. But we generally believe that sex in human beings should be held to a higher standard that supervenes upon biological urges and is equally ingrained in our nature.

However defined, this standard proclaims an ethical or metaphysical imperative that transcends the merely physical. At least, that is how the mainstream of Western philosophy and religion has conceived of our sexuality. What lingers, as an open problem, is the possibility that by its very being sex always and invariably thwarts any such moral aspiration. "Sexual love" would then be a contradiction in terms. Kant sought to resolve that problem in his philosophy of sex.

The traditional view of love and compassion treated them as significantly different from sexuality. It placed them in a separate category, one that classifies these affective dispositions as inherently ethical in some, if not all, of their modalities. Just as Luther claimed that human nature precludes the ability to love but still remains accessible to God's love as it joins people in a spiritual unity over and above their mortal finitude, so too did Kant argue that sexuality, even as a part of what is called sexual love, can be condoned only when it exists in the context of a normative state that transforms it into something superior to itself. Kant thought this occurs through the normativity of marital oneness. The contractual mandates of monogamous matrimony, he believed, are capable of making sexuality truly moral as well as truly human.

Attacking the beliefs of Kant as well as Luther, Schopenhauer repudiates their glorification of marriage and of married love in ways that duplicate his assaults on other idealistic notions about interpersonal intimacy. The only kind of love that Schopenhauer deems moral emanates from compassion. His term for this is *Mitleidshaft*, which is usually translated as either *compassionate love* or *loving-kindness*. Though Kant and Schopenhauer are sometimes similar in their views about sex, they differ radically in their ideas about compassion. Schopenhauer takes it to be not only ethical in itself but also the foundation of ethics as a whole. He describes compassion as an affective attachment that imbues moral action, a sense of identity often felt (though also often absent) in our relations with other living creatures. But that puts it in the realm of what Kant called "the heteronomous," which is to say a response that does not devolve from rational principles.

Kant excludes the heteronomous from his definition of morality. What is merely felt, he says, need not be ethical in itself or in its consequences; duty requires obedience to necessary and universal dictates of reason; and so, even a commendable sentiment of benevolence or compassion does not provide an adequate explanation of moral conduct. At that point, Kant and Schopenhauer are worlds apart.

In this and the next chapter I will be asking the following questions related to these matters: How does Kant's moral theory intersect with his ideas about the nature of sex, love, and compassion? Does Schopenhauer correctly perceive the total burden of Kant's ethical philosophy, and does he himself give an acceptable analysis of compassion? How are both philosophers liable to criticism that will enable us to get beyond each of them? And can we thereby attain an outlook, preferable to theirs, that might possibly reveal how either sex or love or compassion may be authentically moral?

Approaching these problems as I do, I amplify my attempts in previous writings to show that the different types of affect are internally related to each other. I made that claim in *Sex: A Philosophical Primer*. In this book I wish to see whether a critical reading of Kant and Schopenhauer can further that speculation on my part.

To carry out this inquiry, I will have to examine Kant's ideas about respect, beneficence, and the kingdom of ends, as well as sex and marriage. Since Kant believed in the goodness of compassionate love and what he nominates as "human love," these too must be studied in connection with his general theory of ethics. It will also be useful to compare the views of Kant and Schopenhauer with those of Rousseau and Hume. In this chapter I concentrate on Kant's philosophy of sexuality.

❄

In his *Lectures on Ethics*, delivered between 1775 and 1780, Kant raises basic questions about the possible morality of what is usually called sexual love. He begins by stating that the notion would seem to be self-contradictory. Human love, Kant argues, is concerned with the welfare of the loved one. It is a state in which people recognize their mutual equality as human beings, each an end in him- or herself, each an autonomous totality, each a person rather than a thing, and therefore someone who must not be used merely for the sake of anyone's selfish desire. Kant defines human love or affection as "the love that wishes well, is amicably disposed, promotes the happiness of others and rejoices in it." But it is wholly clear, he then remarks, that "those who merely have sexual inclination love the person from none of the foregoing motives. . . . In loving from sexual inclination, they make the other into an object of their appetite. . . . The sexual impulse . . . taken in and by itself, is nothing more than appetite."[1]

This entails that sex is not only different from human love, but also in conflict with it. And while human love is moral insofar as it expresses a good will and a concern about another person's well-being, sexual love cannot be moral. In itself, in its basic structure, it is necessarily immoral, as any attempt to reduce a person to a thing would have to be. Moreover, Kant asserts, sexuality is "the only case in which a human being [in his or her totality] is designed by nature as the Object of another's enjoyment."[2]

In saying this, Kant maintains that sexuality is a means of *enjoying* another person. But he scarcely clarifies his concept of enjoyment. He primarily wishes to establish that far from being just an interest in a bit of flesh or region within another's body, sexual desire seeks to render a man or woman into an object of one's selfish gratification, as if he or she were, as a totality, nothing but a thing.

Kant concludes that in itself sexuality is always a degradation of one's nature. It is not a uniting of human beings but rather a device that reduces them to what he calls their purely genital aspect. "The desire of a man for a woman is not directed to her as a human being; on the contrary, the woman's humanity is of no concern to him, and the only object of his desire is her sex."[3]

From this alone, it follows that sexuality must be immoral. Since love is good will, a humane and benevolent concern about another's welfare, no such thing as ethical sexual love would seem to be a possibility. Kant holds something much more extreme than the commonplace belief that *by* itself, apart from other interests people have, unadulterated sex cannot be moral. He makes the stronger claim that *in* itself sexuality is immoral and debasing to all participants. Still he insists upon the importance of combining sexual desire with human love. To demonstrate how this miraculous feat may occur, he presents a theory of marriage that is as extravagant and idealistic as anything that the nineteenth-century Romantics were later to imagine.

Before examining Kant's solution, we should consider the way he formulated the issue about sexual love in the first place. When Kant declares that through sexuality one enjoys another person, he introduces three different ideas: first, that sexual desire is the only desire that directs itself toward the totality of a human being; second, that, even as an effort to enjoy someone, sexual desire is not a means of delighting in him or her; and third, that sexual desire is appetitive in a manner that is comparable to appetites like hunger or thirst. As a generalization about the nature of sexuality, each of these statements is false, although the second one includes a proposition that is both true and significant.

It is false to say that by its nature sexuality is appetitive, if in saying this we imply—as Kant does—that on all occasions, inevitably and uniformly, it seeks to appropriate other persons for the benefit of one's own organic needs. Hunger and thirst are appetites of that sort. We reach into the refrigerator and devour a chicken for no reason other than our wanting to gratify our desire for nourishment or gustatory pleasure. We do not care about the chicken as an end that has, or rather once had, vital interests of its own. If we had had that concern, the chicken might never have ended up in the refrigerator.

At times sexual desire is undoubtedly appetitive in that sense. Men and women are not infrequently motivated by physiological forces that cause them to hunger for anyone or anything that will satisfy their hormonal sex drive. But though this is a part, and often a major part, of human sexuality, it does not characterize all of sex or exclude components of a different type. Kant makes a fundamental mistake in not recognizing this.

We need not linger here on the extent to which human sexuality is appetitive. On numerous occasions it may even differ only slightly from hunger and thirst. What really matters is whether it always resembles them, and whether the degree and frequency of resemblance are sufficient for us to treat it as a comparable mode of appropriation and self-gratification. Kant's underlying presupposition about the character of this resemblance is what I wish to repudiate.

In many, perhaps most, instances, sexual appetite reveals an attitude toward its object that has no counterpart in hunger or thirst. The person one desires is usually seen to have human characteristics that are like our own, or at least complementary to them. Normally we do not yearn for the enjoyment of another's genitalia, but rather for direct, albeit physical, intimacy with that other person. If people were sexless and had no genitalia, we might not have erotic or libidinal feelings in relation to them. All the same, our sexual feelings are ordinarily directed toward more than just their genitals, or any other portion of their body.

To this extent, the appetitiveness of human sexuality is unlike the appetitiveness of hunger and thirst. A craving for roast chicken is the strongly felt activation of alimentary processes that are capable of quieting stomach pangs once the food has been ingested. Sex is not like that. Even when it is highly goal-oriented, it generally lusts after a someone, whether in imagination or actuality, who is the man or woman that arouses mental and physical excitation in us. Our attention may become fixated upon a particular erotogenic zone; but the carnality of the other person is rarely desired for itself alone.

As Kant errs in thinking that sexuality is merely appropriative, so too is he mistaken when he claims that it, and only it, addresses itself to the totality of other persons. For one thing, are we sure we know what such an attitude would be like? How might one describe the entirety of a person we desire? Does it comprise all of that individual's past and future attributes, or is it only what he or she is at the moment? And if the latter, where do we draw the line between relevant and irrelevant properties of this man or woman? Can Kant possibly mean that sexual desire includes an interest in the veins and inner organs that operate within someone's body, or the welter of perceptions, sensations, thoughts, fears, hopes, and varied feelings that throng within his or her consciousness and overall personality? In our effort to enjoy another human being as a totality, what exactly are we trying to enjoy? And why believe that sex is the means, the only means, by which this enjoyment can occur?

While I find these questions somewhat unmanageable, and most likely unanswerable, I realize that people can have a vaguely panoramic attachment to someone who is experienced not as a composite of different attributes but as a complete and whole individual. A man who is attracted by a woman's physical appearance may be responding to more than just her embodiment of sexual beauty. His impulse might be focused upon her particular features because they belong to *her*, as the person whose intimate presence he desires. And perhaps that is why Kant thought that sexual feeling is a yearning to enjoy the totality of another.

But he never tells us what this means, and anyhow it runs counter to his belief that sex is an appetite like hunger or thirst. Though these can be directed toward parts of an object as well as its totality, they are not means of enjoying it *as* a totality. On the other hand, when sex is appetitive in the way that hunger and thirst are, which happens in solitary masturbation or limiting situations where people exist for each other as little more than sexual outlets, enjoying a person in his or her totality does not seem to be what is going on.

Nevertheless, Kant is right, I believe, insofar as he implies that sex is a means of enjoying persons. As we variably enjoy listening to music, or watching a tennis match, or having a lively conversation, or taking a walk in springtime, so too can we enjoy persons in responses that are distinctively sexual. Interpersonal enjoyment of any sort is not the same as taking delight in or wishing well. The latter are more selfless than enjoyment, especially sexual enjoyment, since they are exclusively concerned about what is good for the other. At the same time, enjoying a person is not equivalent to using him or her for one's own personal benefit, or for just the satisfying of one's hedonic needs. To enjoy another person is to feel comfort and renewed well-being in associating with this man or woman, and sometimes a sense of oneness with him or her. Through a bond that we welcome as a good thing, we draw sustenance from the other without diminishing either of us. Our ability to enjoy each other augments the being of us both. It is an enrichment in which we partake jointly.

Suggestive though it may be, Kant's notion of sex as an attempt to enjoy another person is tainted by his belief that only in sex do we seek such enjoyment. That is not the case. We enjoy people across a vast gamut of affective experiences. The search for interpersonal enjoyment plays a major role in relations of nonsexual love, of friendliness as well as friendship, or of any affirmative response to a person's beauty, charm, cheerfulness, elegance, wit, intelligence, moral character, and artful self-presentation. As a means of uniting with someone, sexual desire—in its most common occurrence—is the longing by a human being to establish vibrant contact through enjoyment of the body and living presence of some other person. Moreover, a man or woman we desire sexually can also represent, or symbolize, or serve as surrogate for, various people who have had importance in our past experience, and within the many stages of our developmental growth.

The traits or bodily features that are sexually enjoyable need not be related to anything genital. A man can desire a woman because she is gracious in her movements, has a mellifluous voice and lovely eyes, perhaps, or because she is intellectually brilliant but also mysterious. Not much, if any, of this may be traceable to the physiology of reproductive instincts; yet it all pertains to the person that woman is or appears to be. It reveals what a man may wish to enjoy, though not necessarily to appropriate, by means of sexual closeness to her. Like most of the other ways that people can be enjoyed, doing so through sexuality is interwoven with everything else that matters to human beings. It is operative in accordance with their individual system of values.

As I have suggested, and as Kant also mentions, enjoying a person is not the same as delighting in that person. This is a confusion that Diderot makes in formulating his concept of *jouissance* (enjoyment), which Kant may have been thinking about.[4] But here again, Kant's seminal idea remains undeveloped. To delight in someone is to feel joy in what he or she is and does, apart from whatever we ourselves enjoy or desire. The feeling of delight is an expression of aesthetic, and often moral, approbation. It readily mingles with dispassionate, though receptive, acceptance of the person who has elicited our joyful response. While we may delight in people we enjoy, provided the enjoyment is sufficiently inclusive of what is good for them, we can enjoy a person without delighting in him or her.

Enjoying is also different from liking. To like a person is to like some of the attributes that constitute what he or she is. But however greatly we may enjoy a person because of properties we like in him or her, it is not the same as enjoying either the properties or the totality of that person. Enjoying people is similar to enjoying good health or the commendation of those whose opinion means something to us. It is life-enhancing, and therefore more conducive to mutual happiness than merely liking someone. Had Kant recognized this, he might not have assumed that sexual enjoyment is inherently inimical to delighting in the welfare and respect that its chosen object deserves insofar as it is a person and not a thing.

Kant fails to understand the kind of enjoyment and delight that sexual acuity may create because he thinks sexuality inevitably treats the other person as an object of selfish appetite. And if it did entail, necessarily and as a matter of definition, acting toward people as if they were things—just

instrumentalities for satisfying one's own desire—Kant
would be right to see a moral antithesis between sex and
human love. As he says, love (at least the love of persons)
involves good will and a benevolent disposition toward its
recipient as an end in him- or herself. Love not only delights
in, but also fosters, another's search for consummation
without rendering that person into something we use simply
for our own purposes.

By denying that sexuality violates the conditions needed
for human love to exist, we can explain the possible
affiliation between sex and love more easily than Kant does.
Sexual love, the conjunction and genuine harmonization of
sex and love, occurs on some, even many, occasions of sexual
desire, though certainly not on all of them. There is thus no
antinomy to be overcome, and no reason to believe that in
itself sexuality is basically immoral.

The approach that I am following is coherent with
statements about sexual love which Hume enunciates in *A
Treatise of Human Nature*. He there suggests that "the
amorous passion, or love betwixt the sexes" is composed of
three elements: "the pleasing sensation arising from beauty;
the bodily appetite for generation; and a generous kindness
or good-will."[5] Though Hume points out that lust, the
bodily appetite, can sometimes conflict with the good intent
of generous kindness, he maintains that in sexual love the
three components are "inseparable." This alone assures the
potential morality of sex. When love occurs, even one "who
is enflamed by lust, feels at least a momentary kindness
towards the object of it, and at the same time fancies her
more beautiful than ordinary; as there are many, who begin
with kindness and esteem for the wit and merit of the
person, and advance from that to the other passions."[6]

Hume credits the sense of beauty with making the amorous state into a humane and ethical condition. He says that it unites lust with kindness, and therefore sex with love. It alters the nature of the two other elements and produces sexual love when it "diffuses" through them both.

Kant knew Hume's work and could have availed himself of its benign and wholesome implications. They seem to have had no effect upon him.

❄

Deriving from his presuppositions about sex, Kant's solution in terms of marriage is equally dubious. Seeking a viable relationship within which human beings might relate to one another sexually without their being treated as things because of their sexuality, Kant infers that only monogamous matrimony can meet these requirements. No other arrangement is moral.

Kant finds prostitution and free love immoral because, by their very nature, they preclude what is needed for there to be morality in sex. Prostitution implies that a person is renting out his or her body for sexual purposes as if it were property to be disposed of like any other. But our body is so intimately related to our personality, Kant asserts, that such employment means treating another, and/or oneself, as if he or she were not a person but only a thing. Even where carnal pleasures are freely exchanged, Kant believes that the ingredient desires remain geared to the using of someone as a thing to be possessed. He insists that unmarried lovers who engage in sexual behavior cannot truly respect the humanity in each other.

At times Kant reaches similar conclusions on the grounds that having sex for its own sake involves treating another or oneself as a thing because an activity of this sort, seeking only the gratification of our desires, opposes "the natural law." That adheres to the biological purpose for which sex exists, and Kant says it transcends "mere animal pleasure."[7] To lend some credibility to his belief, he would have to demonstrate that the pursuit of sexual pleasures in and for themselves is not only "unnatural" in human beings but also such as to prevent the participants from being treated as persons. Kant gives no such demonstration, and I do not see how he could make a convincing argument along those lines.

Kant's assertions in this regard may seem odd, indeed outrageous, to us two hundred years later. Do they not ignore the fact that liberated sex, but also prostitution, can include authentic concern about the other person? And are we willing to assume that autonomy belonging to personhood is threatened by either commercialized or freely bestowed sexuality apart from marriage? Are we not morally free to use our body as we wish, provided that no one is thereby harmed? If a man sells his plasma to a blood bank, or contributes it as a gratuity, is he treating his body and therefore himself as merely a thing? Most people nowadays would answer in the negative. And should we not say the same about sex? In an obvious sense, sex is a more personal deployment of one's body than the giving of blood, but why consider that pertinent to the matter at hand?

Kant recommends marriage as the sole moral agency of sex because he thinks that only marriage enables people to give each other the respect that human beings deserve, while also gratifying their instinctual needs. How then is sexuality compatible with respect as he defines it, and how does respect transform the immorality of mere sex into the morality of human love ideally present in matrimony?

According to Kant, only if we have a right over another person can we have a right to use that person's sexuality for our own selfish benefit. But we cannot legitimately acquire such rights unless we agree that the other person shall have the same rights over us. This comes into being through the contractual institution that is marriage. Only in marriage does this occur, Kant argues, for only then do we exchange the crucial rights in a situation that unites our autonomous wills. Spousal unity is the sole circumstance he envisages in which people exchange equal and reciprocal rights to their entire person. Being more thoroughly interpersonal than any other, the marital commitment provides a couple with total and mutual access to each other's body. Since husband and wife possess identical rights to the total being of each other, their relationship conduces to no reduction of personhood, no disrespect, no misuse of the humanity in either of them.

The consummation of sexuality in legal and functional matrimony is moral, Kant concludes, because the surrendering of rights through marriage does not entail any ultimate loss: "If I yield myself completely to another and obtain the person of the other in return, I win myself back; I have given myself up as the property of another, but in turn I take that other as my property, and so win myself back again in winning the person whose property I have become."[8]

Kant does not venture into the question of what constitutes a happy or desirable marriage. Like everyone else, he knows that successful matrimony largely depends upon psychological attunement between the spouses and their capacity to please each other. He is not inspecting the elements and criteria of a fully commendable marriage. Nor is he considering the fact that marriages very often turn out to be disastrous, which he himself emphasizes in his anthropological writings. As a moralist, he concerns himself only with the ability of the marital bond to make sexual love both human and ethical.

What would otherwise be immoral because it reduces persons to things is thus subsumed within a moral relationship predicated upon reciprocal rights. For sexual love to be a confluence of human love and sexuality it must enact an interest in the welfare of the other person. But only marriage can do that, since only it provides an exchange of reciprocal rights which overcomes the underlying selfishness in sex. Consequently, marriage, and nothing else, makes possible the kind of sexual love that Kant considers worthy of a human being. "In this way," he informs us, "the two persons become a unity of will. Whatever good or ill, joy or sorrow befall either of them, the other will share in it."[9]

That Kant should end up with a description of sexual or married love as a union of wills comes as no surprise. A similar conception was long since built into the wedding service of Western religions. It issues from the biblical portrayal of husband and wife as "one flesh," which John Milton interpreted as meaning "one heart, one soul" and Shakespeare called the "marriage of true minds." Like Milton and Shakespeare, Kant knows that a union of wills implies friendship between those who participate in it. The ideal of friendship itself he depicts as a oneness similar to marriage insofar as each friend surrenders his happiness to the other's keeping but then is completely recompensed because the friend is doing likewise.

In several books I have criticized the notion that human beings can merge or fuse or have a union of wills in this fashion. I argued at length that love demands a different type of unity—an acceptance of another person and a sharing of oneself, but not a fusion of identities.[10] The concept of merging became a major factor in Romantic theories of love in the nineteenth and early twentieth century. Kantian philosophy was foundational to much of the thought about love that developed then.[11]

What rubs most against the current grain is Kant's assurance that a union of wills results from the marital contract itself. His reasoning would seem to be impaled upon an equivocation. Though he is referring to a bond in which the spouses share in the good or ill, the joy or sorrow, of each other, he gives us no grounds for thinking that this must result from marriage as he defines it. The marital relation may establish a giving of equal and reciprocal rights to one's person. But it does not follow that such reciprocity alone leads to an authentic union of wills, or to any comparable sharing of goods, evils, joys, and sorrows. Though the sharing and the relevant oneness can occur, Kant makes hardly any attempt to show how they might be essential components of the married state. Consequently, it is not only his view of marriage that is suspect but also his belief that the humanization and morality of sexual love is possible only in the context of marriage.

In Kant's defense, one could take him as meaning that moral sexual love presupposes a reciprocation of good will, which cannot exist unless rights of access are jointly exchanged, and that this requires a legal—therefore ethical—union of the sort that (monogamous) marriage is. Kant would then be interpreted as affirming only that marriage is a necessary condition for the morality of sexual love, but not a sufficient condition. In other words, there would have to be further conditions as well in order for human love to occur between the sexually active spouses.

This more moderate approach is not, however, what Kant intends. He proposes the stronger, less tenable, conception because he wants to argue that *in itself,* as the institution that it is, marriage joins people in an ethical as well as sexual unity. But that begs the question. Kant does nothing to support any such assumption, though even the lesser claim—in terms of marriage as a necessary condition—needs substantiation on its own.

Finally, we should note how Kant articulates the notion of granting equal and reciprocal rights. He speaks of each member of the marriage "undertaking to surrender" the whole of his or her person, both being willing to "yield [themselves] completely." He holds that the rights at stake are not suitably exchanged unless husband and wife sacrifice their interests and themselves in a total submission to each other. But must self-abnegation of this sort, however mutual and freely undertaken, be part of our definition of the marital bond? Is this self-sacrificial attitude a prerequisite for the creation of a moral relationship between spouses who have sex with each other? Is it a worthy, or even feasible, means of uniting them as beings whose autonomy must be respected?

My own intuitions tell me that the answer to these questions is "Surely not." Marriage and the advent of sexual love as something ethical presuppose a mutual giving of rights, but not of the calculated and legalistic kind that Kant invokes. For one thing, there is no way that we could determine whether all the rights a spouse bestows are truly and identically restored. What, in fact, would this mean? If the wife gives her husband the right to caress her shoulders, which he likes to do, must he give her the right to caress his, which he does not like? In mutual married love, as in mutual love as a whole, there has to be an equalization of rights inasmuch as each person must be concerned about the well-being of the other. But this is quite different from the idea of exchanging rights in a manner that somehow returns to oneself whatever one has given up. Long before Kant, that concept appeared in the writings on love by Marsilio Ficino. It is as fanciful in Kant as it was in Ficino.[12]

Kant depicts marriage as a joint subservience in which each occasion of surrender or renunciation is finally justified by the restitution the other person makes through his or her correlative surrender and renunciation. But then, one may reply, as Nietzsche does, that it is through self-fulfillment, rather than self-submission, that spousal ties can serve as a moral and jointly beneficial bond. Without mentioning Kant, Nietzsche has his doctrine of marital union in mind when he ridicules those who extol an "equal will to renunciation." As he puts it: "If both partners felt impelled by love to renounce themselves, we should then get—I do not know what; perhaps an empty space?"[13]

The emptinesses in Kant's conception of marriage and its dependence upon a contractual exchange of rights may well be irremediable. His idea of human love as goodwill and an interest in the welfare of the beloved is defensible as far as it goes. But it does not go far enough to explain what love is like, either in sexuality or in other social relations. While much that is admirable in romanticism stems from Kant's philosophy, a better account of how sexuality can be an ethical possibility exceeds the cramped parameters that he imposes.

❊

In the chapter that follows this one, I will study Schopenhauer's critique of Kant's metaphysics of morals in an effort to profit from them both. But first I want to discuss briefly a contemporary resuscitation of the Kantian position. Until recently, technical philosophers tended to ignore Kant's writings about sex and marriage. His contractarian approach is reborn, however, in an article by Bernard H. Baumrin entitled "Sexual Immorality Delineated." Like Kant, Baumrin begins with the assertion that "human sexual interaction is essentially manipulative."[14] From this, Baumrin concludes:

first, that it is a mistake to think that sexual intimacy is what he calls "a romance between feelings, where feelings have been elevated to a sacrosanct position," and second, that sex avoids being necessarily immoral only when each participant acknowledges that his or her desire to manipulate initiates not only a corresponding right to manipulate in the other but also a duty to submit to such manipulation.[15]

Against Baumrin, as against Kant, one can respond that it is erroneous to think of sex as *essentially* manipulative. If that were the case, sexuality would have to be considered selfish on each and every occasion, whether or not it becomes moral through contractual devices that create rights and duties.

We avoid this baleful paradox by characterizing interpersonal sex as neither selfish nor manipulative in its very nature, but rather as part of our reaching out for connection and communication with other human beings. Sexual love, and therefore sexual morality, differs from rectitude in business or administration inasmuch as it provides an attunement between people and their responses to each other without any formalistic adjudication of personal desires. Contracts exist as a means of controlling our self-oriented motivation, and one might conceivably think that this applies to sex as it does to other pursuits. But since sexuality is to some degree a vehicle of our yearning for persons who matter to us and with whom we want to make sensory contact, it belongs to a different region of moral discourse.

In part, at least, sex is indeed a "romance between feelings," even though this aspect of it may sometimes be minimal or such as to present itself in a crude, distorted, or abusive fashion. Sexual feelings—whether they be libidinal or erotic or romantic in my use of those terms—are not sacrosanct, but they are too subtle and too pervasive as manifestations of our humanity to be encompassed by contractarian interpretations. The promises we make, the expectations we arouse, the invitations we extend, the behavior we engage in are all social acts, and as such they can be subject to the mandates of a contract. But the feelings expressed by these acts are aesthetic phenomena that have a goodness and a badness all their own. Their "romance" is the narrative of our immediate experience as we live it from moment to moment. That is why fictional works of art are supremely adept at conveying the nature and the affective meaning of sexuality as well as love.

Once we free ourselves from the notion that sex is always and ineluctably manipulative, once we recognize that frequently it is a gratifying search for someone we do not wish to manipulate and may even want to strengthen as an autonomous person, there can be no valid reason to think that its ethical potentiality resides within the dictates of a contract. The character and justifiability of either married or sexual love must depend upon other considerations.[16]

2

The Morality of
Compassion: Contra Kant
and Schopenhauer

In seeking to overcome the dilemma about sexual love, Kant does not offer a separate metaphysics of either sex or love. Instead his analysis draws exclusively upon ethical principles that he derives from his metaphysics of morals. By way of contrast, Schopenhauer devotes a major chapter of *The World as Will and Representation* to what he calls "the metaphysics of love between the sexes." As it turns out, Schopenhauer's metaphysics of love is also a metaphysics of sex. In fact, Schopenhauer reduces love of almost every kind to sex, which he calls the ultimate force that motivates all reality known to beings such as we. But Schopenhauer also has a metaphysics of morality, based upon his ideas about compassion. He uses those ideas to repudiate Kant's ethical theory as a whole. In the process, he implicitly provides a devastating critique of the Kantian conception of compassion as well as love in general.

Schopenhauer's discussion of Kantian ethics appears most fully in his book *On the Basis of Morality*. In it he traces ethical behavior to an impulse of compassion, which he defines as comprising two fundamental virtues: justice and loving-kindness. The former is negative inasmuch as it ordains merely that we do no unnecessary harm to others. The positive aspect of compassion appears in loving-kindness. According to Schopenhauer, only that makes us care about the welfare of other creatures; and it does so without considering how our own personal interests may or may not be furthered by this attitude.

Both justice and loving-kindness counteract the selfishness that Schopenhauer considers unavoidable in purposive existence. He extols justice and loving-kindness as bulwarks against the malice and vicious cruelty that are often present in relations among human beings, and in our species' treatment of other animals. Selfishness being essential for survival, he is stunned and bemused by the fact that people are even capable of experiencing loving-kindness, or compassion of any type. Nevertheless, he claims it is the source of all morality to which we can aspire.

Throughout his argument, Schopenhauer recognizes that loving-kindness also has survival value for our species—it leads us to help other people stay alive. Though its sheer existence is a mystery, he describes it as an innate tendency in everyone. While being neither invariable nor even predictable in our behavior, it seems to him uniquely indicative of what human beings can achieve through morality. As opposed to Kant's attempt to delineate purely rational foundations of ethics, Schopenhauer insists that conscience originates from the wholly adventitious development of compassionate feeling in the social organisms we happen to be. Only by reference to compassion, he believes, can one explain how and why people construct the systems of law and duty that constitute whatever moral code they accept.

Schopenhauer's rejection of the Kantian position is predicated upon his naturalistic approach to life. Had he lived a hundred years later, he might well have espoused current sociobiological theory as a prerequisite to any valid understanding of ethical conduct. He argues that each of the two major formulations of Kant's moral philosophy is false to empirical observation as well as being inconsistent within itself. He reviles both the categorical imperative and the notion that virtuous behavior is by definition the treating of another person as an end and not as a means only.

Schopenhauer attacks the Kantian conception of duty as a prior principle based on abstract rationality by claiming that the doctrine of the categorical imperative is circular. He maintains that it presupposes—instead of proving—the existence of an objective moral law, which reason then purports to have discovered. In actual experience, he says, there is no such objectivity to be found, since commendable acts always spring from some relevant feeling, either directly or indirectly. Schopenhauer is not entirely dismissive of Kant's second principle, about dealing with others as ends in themselves, but he tries to show that it cannot be defended except as a prudential maxim. In his estimation, it reduces to the Golden Rule, which tells us to treat other people as we would want to be treated by them.

For his part, Kant does not deny that compassion has a role in the moral life. He assigns it to the same heteronomous class as the feelings of benevolence and beneficence. According to him, these are all affective responses that may be praiseworthy, and even conducive to the welfare of humanity, but not necessarily moral. He denies that they define the grounding or inner constitution of ethical conduct. They do not address themselves to the fact that the recipient of their goodwill is a rational being capable of self-legislation and therefore free to choose his or her own destiny. Benevolence is a feeling of sympathy or commiseration with another; beneficence is a disposition to take action that

ameliorates the other's condition. Neither concerns itself
with the ability, innately human, to exercise one's freedom of
choice. As a result, Kant asserts, neither in itself can reveal
the nature of morality or what it is to be a person.

To explain the purely ethical dimensions of our being, Kant
invokes the concept of respect. In showing respect, we relate
to someone *as* a person, as a rational entity who can perceive
the difference between right and wrong and who is aware of
being responsible for what he or she freely chooses to do and
become. In effect, Kant defines duty in terms of respect for
the ineluctable autonomy that other people have just as we do.
The second principle of morality manifests the implications
of responding to someone as an end in that sense, while the
first principle formulates the role of rationality in any ethical
decision. Since feelings like compassion have no necessary
relationship to respecting a person as an end, they cannot be
the basis of morality or help us determine what is morally
defensible in the affective attachments that human beings
enter into.

Before trying to resolve this dispute, I want to consider
more carefully the second of the two principles in Kant's
metaphysics of morals. It runs as follows: "So act that you
use humanity, whether in your own person or in the person
of any other, always at the same time as an end, never
merely as a means."[1]

For the last two hundred years that maxim has had for
millions of people the force of established certitude in ethics.
Can anyone nowadays question its cogency? It has often been
misrepresented by those who forget the importance that the
word *merely* plays in it. Kant never doubts, indeed always
stresses, the fact that we all serve as means for each other. As
participants in the universal struggle to exist, we do and must

use others as if they were commodities that can further our own well-being. Whether or not we admit it, they are to us more than independently autonomous persons. However great her love may be, a mother needs her child just as the child needs its mother. They may not feel an equal or identical love, and rarely do their individual experiences have the same components or intensity. Yet their feelings are alike inasmuch as both types of attachment involve some recognition by each that the person one cares about as an end in his- or herself is also a means to what will benefit oneself. By introducing *merely* or related words into the ethical mandate, Kant incorporates these comprehensive conditions but goes far beyond them.

This "beyond" is the realm of personhood to which all people belong indefeasibly. Persons, human beings as a whole, cannot be reduced to things. Regardless of how they may be treated—or, for that matter, how they treat themselves—an attempt to render persons into things, commodities and nothing else, is always immoral. That is the burden of Kant's ethical theory, and I myself do not find this part of his view mistaken or at all troublesome. In itself, it seems to me the beginning of wisdom about morality. Schopenhauer failed to appreciate its great import.

Difficulties arise, however, as soon as we consider the ramifications of Kant's approach. To begin with, his substantive principle is arbitrarily circumscribed in its extension. It addresses itself to humanity alone, as if our species—and *only* our species—can be its primary concern. Though his terminology is a little misleading, Kant is not referring to the human race in abstraction from the persons who show it forth, but to human beings themselves as distinct from other living creatures. Even animals that are biologically close to us, the other primates for instance, are denied the moral protection embodied in Kant's second principle. They are not given shelter within its precious domain. As we shall see, Kant compensates for this shortcoming by saying that nonhuman animals should be treated in some respects *as if* they were persons. But this indirection in his theory creates problems of its own, and, as I will suggest, they may be devastating to his entire outlook.

Being human-centric, Kant's ethical theory has a corresponding narrowness in its denotation of personhood. Despite the plenitude of candidates for that distinctive appellation, only men and women and their children are said to be worthy of being characterized literally as persons. Kant defends this restriction by claiming that members of other species do not have the inborn capacity to discern or act upon the necessary and universal standards that underlie the making of moral decisions.

This aptitude of reasoning and self-regulation is not only the prior condition for anyone to be ethical and to have a good will, Kant holds, but also it demarcates the class of animate beings to which we can possibly accord moral rights. However much chimpanzees or domestic pets may resemble us, he insists that we anthropomorphize them foolishly if we think they can have the kind of rationality that enables people to be autonomous ends in themselves, to carve out their own destiny, and to possess an ethical status that must be recognized and respected. Only we who are human can be liable to the praise or condemnation that this involves. Only we can achieve the dignity that results from living in accordance with morals that we legislate for ourselves through our powers of rationality. Since other animals lack any such potential, Kant denies them access to the fundamental rights that people have. Nonhuman creatures are not to be considered the same as tables and chairs, but neither should we attribute personhood to them or think that they—any more than tables or chairs—can belong to the kingdom of ends that morality encloses.

These Kantian beliefs are correct to the extent that members of other species are comparable to things in lacking the cognitive resources needed to make ethical choices. Of course, human beings are also limited in that respect when their minds are either undeveloped or impaired by circumstances, whether permanent or temporary, that we deem foreign to their nature. Kant's principle accommodates such qualifications. But even so, he fails to note how thoroughly the personhood that is available to humankind resembles the experience and behavior of many animals. In the twenty-first century we feel uncomfortable with the arrogance of his proclamation that we alone should count as persons while all the others must be analogous to material objects. As far as anyone can tell, only we have the requisite *conception*, the abstract idea, of ethical standards, as only we can imagine the square root of a negative number. But this does not justify the belief that all other creatures may be used as we use things, and therefore without our being obligated to have any direct concern about the morality of *how* we use them.

We can therefore agree with Schopenhauer when he complains that there are no sufficient grounds for Kant to suggest that only human beings should be treated as ends rather than as means merely. At the same time, we may still affirm the fundamental difference between persons and things. There is certainly some basis for doing so. But the character of the distinction will have changed. It will now be seen as allowing a significant moral overlap between the different types of animate entities, an overlap that Kant scarcely admits.

Once we make this move, we liberate ourselves from Kant's emphasis upon rationality. He himself remarks that human beings are like other animals in seeking happiness and whatever gratifications that nature makes possible in us as well as them. Nevertheless, by maintaining that ethical rectitude means acting from duty, which is to say, in accordance with principles that exist only in rational beings, he ignores the fact that the quest for happiness and fulfillment permeates our existence more or less the way it does in the rest of animality. If we limit human personhood to its sheer rationality, in the manner of Kantian ethics, we commit an intellectual sin against nature.

As if to do penance for this sin, Kant introduces compensatory ideas about the love of nonhuman animals. In a brief chapter that discusses duties toward them, he starts by asserting that there can be no such duties directly, but only indirectly:

> Animals are not self-conscious and are there merely as means to an end. That end is man. We can ask, "Why do animals exist?" But to ask, "Why does man exist?" is a meaningless question. Our duties towards animals are merely indirect duties towards humanity. . . . Thus, if a dog has served his master long and faithfully, his service, on the analogy of human service, deserves reward, and when the dog has grown too old to serve, his master ought to keep him until he dies. Such action helps to support us in our duties towards human beings, where they are bounden duties. . . . If a man shoots his dog because the animal is no longer capable of service, he does not fail in his duty to the dog, for the dog cannot judge, but his act is inhuman and damages in himself that humanity which it is his duty to show towards mankind.[2]

This would seem to show a lack of true concern about the dog itself, even though Kant states that, by analogy to a human being, the animal deserves to be rewarded. Schopenhauer characterizes Kant's attitude toward animals as "revoltingly crude, a barbarism of the West."[3] He cites a passage in which Kant points out that cruelty to animals deadens our sympathy for their sufferings but then goes on to say that this is immoral because it weakens "a natural tendency that is very useful to morality in relation to other human beings."[4] He takes Kant to mean that "only for practice are we to have sympathy for animals." Schopenhauer regards that as "abominable."[5]

In context, however, Kant's statement can be read differently. Just after the passage I have quoted, he remarks that "the more we come in contact with animals and observe their behaviour, the more we love them, for we see how great is their care of their young. . . . Tender feelings towards dumb animals develop humane feelings towards mankind."[6]

In placing this commendation of love for animals next to his denial that we can have direct duties toward them, Kant has two goals in mind. First, he is illustrating his idea that nothing but humanity can be the direct object of our duties, and therefore whatever duties we may have toward animals must be indirect duties toward humanity. But in addition he is explicitly advocating love and other tender feelings in relation to animals. He makes his plea not merely because those feelings are instrumental to the development of a humane attitude toward other people but also because there is something in the being and lifestyle of animals themselves that elicits such responses in us.

Had Kant thought that animals are *only* "man's instruments," he would have had to explain why he believes that using them for sport is reprehensible. He has no inclination to condemn even barbarous sports, wrestling, or bare-fisted prize fighting for example, in which human participants are purveyors of sadistic enjoyment experienced by the spectators. If animals ought to be exempt from such brutalization, as he asserts, the reason must be more than just concern about its indirect effect upon humankind. Though his ethical theory prevents Kant from saying we have any direct duties toward animals, he implies that the nature of their condition as living creatures should nevertheless awaken in us those "tender feelings" to which he refers.

I make these comments in order to suggest that Kant's rationalism retains, as a saving remnant, many of the humanitarian sentiments that he inherited from Rousseau as well as Hume or Shaftesbury and that Schopenhauer wished to accentuate. Kant's "kingdom of ends" is not an ethereal collection of emotionally desiccated rational beings. On the contrary, it is an ideal though possibly unrealizable society of persons imbued with all the vital feelings and cravings for happiness that naturalists in philosophy have always deemed basic in our reality. Kant argues that morality exceeds, but does not eliminate, these considerations. While demanding their subordination to conscience and respect for the autonomy of others, he envisages the good life as a harmonization that can, in principle, include our love of animals as well as other people (and ourselves).

This aspect of Kant's philosophy appears in what he writes about compassion, little of which is mentioned in Schopenhauer's critique. At one point Kant states that "love out of inclination"—what Schopenhauer would call loving-kindness—cannot be commanded, but that kindness done from duty has practical import. The latter resides in the will and infuses moral action; the former issues from propensions of feeling and what Kant calls *"schmelzender Teilnehmung."*[7]

This term is sometimes translated as *tender sympathy*, sometimes as *melting compassion*, and sometimes as *melting sympathy*.[8] In any case, it would seem to imply scorn for a mawkish sentimentality arising from an incorrect view about the nature of morality. But Kant is not maligning sympathy or compassion in themselves. He is condemning only a type of emotionality that may cause them to defy the proper dictates of reason. When that happens, our feelings show insufficient respect for the personhood of whomever they are directed toward. Although this failing is not inevitable, sympathy and compassion remain as heteronomous inclinations that cannot reveal what duty signifies.

Kant's ideas about nonsexual love of others and of humanity at large are more consistent than his critics have sometimes recognized. Even when he observes that people often delude themselves into thinking they are acting out of duty when actually they are following an impulse of love and affection, he does not suggest that their feelings are either immoral or a circuitous means of attaining some egoistic benefit for themselves. He does not deny that loving-kindness is ethical when it conforms to rational principles; he only declares that by itself, as a disposition whose status must always be subject to evaluation, it is not necessarily moral.

In this connection we may profitably juxtapose two statements by Kant that seem to conflict with each other, but do not really. In the *Grounding for the Metaphysics of Morals* he remarks that all inclinations—including those of love or compassion—"are so far from having an absolute value such as to render them desirable for their own sake that the universal wish of every rational being must be, rather, to be wholly free from them."[9] Yet in *Religion Within the Limits of Reason Alone* he affirms something much more humanistic: "Natural inclinations *considered in themselves*, are *good*, that is not a matter of reproach, and it is not only futile to want to extirpate them but to do so would also be harmful and blameworthy."[10]

If natural inclinations are good in themselves and it is blameworthy to want to extirpate them, how can it be possible for rational beings to wish to be wholly free from them? The possibility of inconsistency on Kant's part disappears once we realize that in his first statement the "absolute value" to which he refers would be such as to render natural inclinations ethically desirable under all circumstances and therefore for their own sake alone. But that cannot be, since every inclination has to be adjudged in the court of moral reasoning. And if human nature is as fragile or liable to corruption and self-deception as Kant assumes, he can also surmise that as rational beings we would prefer to be free of desire rather than run the risks entailed by the idea of its being valuable in any absolute sense.

This generalization about what people must or would decide in a case of that sort may be erroneous, even outlandish. It does not, however, contradict Kant's belief that natural desires are good in themselves. He can consistently maintain their inherent goodness inasmuch as that precedes any determination of which among them are either moral or immoral. Apart from the fact that an attempt to destroy all of them is futile, many desires can pass muster on ethical grounds. It would be blameworthy to extirpate these in particular. Love or compassion that is morally justifiable—indirectly though not directly moral in itself—could thus survive unhampered.

Because Kant thinks love that is sympathy or compassion must only be an inclination, not a feeling we can will or treat as something we are obligated to experience, he denies the possibility of an inherent duty to love. The notion that such a duty might exist he calls an "absurdity." But immediately afterward, he reminds us that everyone has a duty on all occasions to bear a good will toward other human beings, and even to do good to them, although it may be true that "our species, on closer acquaintance, is not particularly lovable."[11]

In other words, Kant holds that both benevolence (concern about other people's welfare) and beneficence (acting in an effort to benefit them) are moral duties that impinge upon us all regardless of what our inclinations may or may not be. "Benevolence is satisfaction in the happiness (well-being) of others; but beneficence is the maxim of making others' happiness one's end, and the duty to it consists in the subject's being constrained by his reason to adopt this maxim as a universal law."[12]

To this extent, one might add, compassion toward fellow humans can have a significant role within any possible morality. Kant demarcates its ethical terrain when he suggests that if you do what is good for others your beneficence will create a love of them in you. Since there can be no duty to love, or to have any feeling not itself ordained by reason, this outcome will only be indirectly moral. It is not the basis of morality, but Kant never denies that it is part of what a good life would comprise.

As a way of clarifying the difference between the direct and the indirect aspects of ethical response, Kant describes the former as "the capacity and the will to share in others' feelings," whereas the latter can only be "the receptivity, given by nature itself, to the feeling of joy and sadness in common with others."[13] The first of these attitudes he calls free, since it is willed autonomously though grounded in practical reason and obligatory. The second is unfree but nonobligatory. It is caused by laws of nature and just "spreads naturally among human beings living near one another."[14]

Kant likens this second circumstance to the contagiousness of communicable diseases. His term for it is *Mitleidenschaft*, usually translated as *compassion*. Nevertheless this detail of linguistic usage may not have special importance here, since he depicts the directly moral attitude as *communio sentiendi liberalis* (rendered as *sympathetic* in English). The crucial distinction he has in mind is the one that separates moral attitudes founded on reason alone from those that may be commendable but exist as social feelings that he calls "aesthetic" rather than directly ethical.

In view of this highly nuanced synthesis between the doctrines of Kant's rationalist forebears and the alternative approach of thinkers like Hume, Shaftesbury, and Rousseau, we may wonder about the degree of accuracy in Schopenhauer's critique. Before considering that, however, we need to gauge the philosophical price that Kant must pay in discriminating as he does between direct and indirect morality.

To naive or empirically-minded laymen Kant's fundamental tenet may seem to have little or no relevance for deciding how we ought to live. What effective difference does it make, one may ask, if we say that tender feelings toward an animal or suffering human being are not incumbent upon us "directly" but only "indirectly"? The recipient of our beneficence may not care whether our concern is justifiable as either an expression of our prior duty toward that individual or as an affective gesture that in itself bestows value upon him or her. Kant's assertion that our feelings of benevolence or loving-kindness are not inherently moral when they result from inclination rather than duty might seem to have no concrete importance. In any situation, someone acting on the basis of humanitarian sentiments might end up doing exactly the same thing as another person would who acts conscientiously, from duty, and either with or without the occurrence of those sentiments.

Moreover Kant himself shrewdly notes that we can never know with certainty whether anyone's righteous conduct has been motivated by a sense of duty rather than a selfish motive that may only appear to be dutiful. But if that is true, why should we bother about Kant's arcane—though possibly correct—distinction between direct and indirect types of morality?

By way of reply, Kant could insist that his analysis helps us to understand who in principle is worthy of ethical approbation. If someone does a good thing but not out of duty or a conscientious intent, this person has not earned our moral commendation even if the beneficial act is as it ethically ought to be. From natural inclinations as a whole, Kant would say, one cannot derive the entire class of virtuous behavior that dutiful people undertake *because* they are dutiful. Though our actions may often have a desirable outcome, it would be wrong to think that we ourselves are therefore righteous. As T. S. Eliot puts it, in a slightly different context, the greatest treason is "to do the right deed for the wrong reason."[15]

In opposition to this defense, critics of Kant from Schiller to the present have replied that it seems strange to say that a person of good will, a man or woman who behaves out of humane inclinations and without selfishness, should not be recognized as ethically motivated and therefore morally praiseworthy.[16] Reformulated, such criticism may have some merit. As it stands, it is incomplete. It fails to engage Kant properly if it only makes a counter assertion to the effect that someone merits our moral approbation for having acted because of compassionate feelings. At best, we would only be forced to choose between Kant's assurances and those of Schiller or his successors. But their criticism of Kant becomes more challenging, I believe, if we see it as reopening the entire question of what is meant by morality and what Kant can legitimately achieve by making the sense of duty central in it as he does.

Once we enter that level of discourse, we are immediately confronted by the titles of Kant's two principal works on this topic. One offers itself as a *Grundlagen*, a "grounding" or "groundwork," and the other makes it clear that the investigation is about the *metaphysics* of morals. In each book, Kant seeks to explicate the a priori conditions for there to be any morality whatsoever. Like Schopenhauer, he wants to reveal the basis of morality, what it is that enables morality to be a fundamental constituent of our nature as the beings that we are. This leads him to define humanity in terms of the rationality it shares with no other species, the ultimate autonomy that belongs to us as persons, and the inherent respect that serves as a condition for there to be any ethics that human beings can possibly have. Only duty as something we act *from*, and not just in accordance *with*, accommodates these requirements.

Presented as this kind of metaphysics, nonverifiable as all metaphysics is, Kant's formulation may be highly meaningful for many people. It is nevertheless flawed as a philosophical doctrine. Its weakness consists in its puristic implications. It neglects or minimizes a large segment of the moral plenitude that matters in the moment-by-moment existence of ordinary life.

Even if we limit ourselves to the decisions that magistrates must make, and ought to make with utmost rectitude, Kant's view is only partly applicable. As he rightly asserts, someone who adjudicates a moral issue must not be swayed by natural inclinations of commiseration or melting compassion that he or she may also have. The judge must act as a vehicle of duty, following the dictates of conscience and whatever laws coherently implement them. Without reason, and an unswerving devotion to reason, this cannot occur. And yet, it does not follow that the content of a dutiful attitude consists *only* in acting to create or foster respect for the personhood of rational beings. That is an ideal that some individuals have revered throughout their lives, and it may be accepted as a principle that society should protect and preserve. It is, however, but one among other ideals that human beings care about.

Promoting the welfare, and curtailing the suffering, of other creatures—who may or may not be dignified as having personhood—is also an ideal that can weigh heavily in the scales of morality. The question that Kant must answer is whether his metaphysics makes it more, or possibly less, likely that this philanthropic dimension in human nature will flourish as a viable element of practical behavior. By finding a place in his philosophy for indirect as well as direct duties of human love, Kant presents an affirmative response to this question. But his predilection for rationality and the primacy of acting from duty alone is so rigid, and so remote from the complexity of actual decision making, as to awaken suspicions about his general outlook.

It is here that Schiller's tender-hearted consternation has its undeniable strength. The persistent inwardness of Kant's idealization of duty pervades his thought and often makes his philosophy sound like an effusion of reason imposing a morality geared only to its own interests. To that extent, as I have been suggesting, Kant's rationalism detracts from the more humane elements of his view. Schopenhauer's critique does well to remind us that reason is not the only basis of morality, and that compassion can also claim to be foundational in it. But we must still determine whether the solution that Schopenhauer sketches is by and large preferable to the one that Kant offers.

❄

In studying Schopenhauer on the morality of compassion, we can hasten past his misconceptions of Kant's philosophy. I have already touched on some of them in this chapter. They reappear in relation to adulatory comments about Rousseau that Schopenhauer makes. Calling him "undoubtedly the greatest moralist of modern times," he contrasts Rousseau with Kant and other thinkers who "positively reject and condemn compassion."[17] Not only does this misrepresent the Kantian position, but also it alerts us to the fact that Schopenhauer himself duplicates some of the glaring confusion to be found in Rousseau.

As exemplary texts Schopenhauer quotes passages in French from *Emile* and from the *Discourse on the Origin of Inequality*. The crucial term that figures throughout is *pitié* (pity), for which *commisération* is sometimes substituted. Rousseau claims that all the social virtues emanate from that single feeling. Schopenhauer's agreement with this belief is reinforced by his idea that human existence is basically *Leiden* (suffering), and therefore that the morality of pity consists in its supreme ability to create compassionate identification with other victims in the cosmic horror of life.

Kant had also talked about pity, but he implicitly—though with total awareness, I am sure—described it as something different from compassion. Kant thought that pity is not moral, even indirectly. Through pity we treat another as if he or she is inferior, not equal to us who now deign to commiserate with such a hapless individual. In that event, Kant states, the one who pities looks down on this person and thus fails to accord him or her the respect and recognition of autonomous personhood to which every human being has an unquestionable right. On the other hand, Kant never doubts that in having and carrying out an interest in the welfare of someone else compassion is commendable as an expression of human love. It is, therefore, very different from pity.

Kant's argument seems to me trenchant and correct. Schopenhauer himself modifies his amalgamation of pity and compassion in one interesting qualification that he introduces. While trying to prove that compassion penetrates to another's suffering, as pity also does, he admits a sense in which compassionate concern entails identification with those who experience contentment or good fortune. The same could not be true of pity. But this is a rather minor consideration, Schopenhauer tells us. Since pain and privation are indigenous to the human lot, no type of satisfaction, enjoyment, or happiness can ever be "*positive and directly felt.*" Consequently, "the fortunate and content man *as such* leaves us indifferent really. . . . It is true that we can take pleasure in the good fortune, well-being, and enjoyment of others; but then this is secondary, brought about by the fact that their suffering and privation had previously distressed us."[18]

As a further clarification of this view, Schopenhauer says that we share in the joyful experience of another only because "he is our child, father, friend, relation, servant, subject, and so on."[19] Not only do the contentedness and prosperity of people outside this closed society leave us in "idle unconcern," but "even the sight of success and enjoyment *purely as such* can very easily excite envy, to which everyone is prone."[20]

Rousseau had stated that identification with other persons presupposes that they are not happier than we but only more pitiable. If one defines compassion in this way, however, one is prevented from recognizing, as part of its primary configuration, the vibrant sense of delight and indiscriminate goodwill toward others that people often feel. We identify with strangers as well as friends or relations not only by commiserating with them but also by delighting in them, by participating vicariously in the rewards or serendipities of life that may have befallen them, and by relishing this sense of oneness with them.

Such sentiments are not addressed only to a child or parent or equivalent person, as Schopenhauer believes. We can and do delight in the spontaneous and, as we say, "innocent" vitality that all young animals manifest at one stage or another, and that recurs in achievements of the human spirit at any period of life. Even if the condition of our species is basically suffering and privation, we don't identify with lucky or successful individuals for that reason alone. We also identify with them because we can put ourselves in their position through our imaginative conception of their serendipity as something good or beautiful that we too would like to experience—though we usually know this will never happen.

In reply to my criticism, one might respond that I am now describing a relation that differs from the compassionate attitude. But in his depiction of compassion, even Schopenhauer includes an active concern about the welfare of the other as well as our wanting to alleviate suffering in him or her. Delighting in the image of other people's happiness is not separate from desiring to free them from the misery that would preclude their ever being happy. Since these are polar dispositions, both types of identification must be accepted as defining properties of compassion.

That is why we would wonder about the morality of a man or woman who acts compassionately toward someone in need of help and yet takes no delight in whatever joyful outcome eventuates as a result of his or her intervention. We would suspect that while a benefactor of this sort does the right thing and is motivated by moral sentiment the action and the feeling are tainted by an inability to share in the goodness that has now been made possible for another human being. However philanthropic the benefactor may be, we may justly think that this person's social nature is inadequately developed in some affective region that the compassionate disposition normally entails. The morality of compassion involves both modes of identification, each in tandem with the other.

In another respect, Schopenhauer's characteristic way of depicting compassion must also give us pause. When he describes how it can even occur in creatures who are as selfish as human beings are, he repeatedly remarks that people recognize "the eternal essence that exists in every living thing, and shines forth with inscrutable significance from all eyes that see the sun."[21] Schopenhauer does not explain what this eternal essence is exactly. He thinks we need only look into the eyes of some other animal, even a wild beast, to perceive the essence that shines forth in it. He means that we will apprehend the will to live that surges through every bit of life. His saying this does not trouble me. What I find doubtful is his interpretation of why and how we react to what appears in the eyes of fellow creatures.

Schopenhauer reports that through compassionate identification he feels someone's suffering "as my own, and yet not within me, but in another person."[22] He claims that this experience breaks down the barrier between ego and nonego. We are thus united not only with other persons but also with animate beings that are not persons, and indeed with life as a whole.

Schopenhauer portrays this occurrence as an empirical and frequently observable phenomenon, though mysterious if we assume that selfishness is universal in human nature. To show how it is possible for compassion to take us beyond egoism, he states that in reality all living entities are one being. In *The World as Will and Representation* he argues that individuation is illusory and that we are just manifestations of the unitary Will—the life force as it flows through our existence. In his metaphysics of compassion he applies that doctrine, using it to account for our intuition that other creatures participate in the same eternal essence as we do. It serves as the explanation of our capacity to identify with them through affective and behavioral responses that constitute the compassionate attitude. Beyond our faith in the surface appearance of individuation, compassion is "a reminder of that respect in which we are all one and the same entity."[23]

I have elsewhere criticized this mode of explaining compassion, particularly in relation to the notion of merging or fusion that it presupposes.[24] At present I need only emphasize that, far from establishing compassionate feeling as the basis of morality, it actually undermines Schopenhauer's views about that. If we are all one and the same entity already, how is it even possible for there to be the conflict between selfishness and the compassion that seeks to overcome it? If we are united in reality, why is compassion needed, and how can it be counted as the basis of any supervening morality? On ethical as well as metaphysical grounds, it would seem more obvious and more tenable to think that only in the framework of inescapable individuation does compassion take on its humanistic value and capacity to create moral goodness.

At the same time, I feel the great allure of Schopenhauer's ethics. In arguing that compassion is the source of virtue, and not only indirectly virtuous as Kant ordains, Schopenhauer forces us to reorder our moral priorities. Respect for the rationality in human nature is dethroned in the sense that feelings of love and sympathy as well as compassion itself are proffered as the basic phenomena that determine what are truly ethical relations. These are relations that bind us to all of animality, and perhaps to life in its entirety, distinct individuals though we are within that swirling flux. As such, our sense of identification takes precedence over acting from duty alone, which must itself be shown in every situation to benefit some animate creature.

In saying this, I do not mean that Kant's ideas about the morality of compassion can now be discarded. They are useful as a corrective to Rousseau's, as well as Schopenhauer's, boundless reliance on feeling. Even though compassion is generally commendable, it can also be perverse and harmful, even unethical, in its application. Kant was right in arguing that for reasons of duty, conscience, and respect for the autonomy of other persons, we should resist feelings of tenderness that weaken our resolve to do what we know we ought to do. In and by itself, compassion alone cannot be definitive of morality.

But neither does Kantian rationalism provide sufficient conditions. With his usual wit and biting sarcasm, Schopenhauer hits the nail on the head when he says that every magistrate who acts out of duty and sentences a criminal to prison is thereby using that man or woman as a deterrent to other ne'er-do-wells instead of respecting his or her rational desire to avoid punishment and live freely as an autonomous person. Though this does not prove that compassion is the origin and sole basis of morality, it does give us reason to deny that merely acting from motives of duty is.

As in much of philosophy, the dualism that wrenches these alternatives into antagonistic possibilities should be eschewed. Why must we think that there is only *one* basis of morality? Should we not be searching for the ways in which these two candidates interact, more or less coherently though always being capable of diverging on some occasion?

If we accept this pluralistic stance, we may also perceive that compassion, and respect as well, has a role to play throughout the morality of all affect in human life. The morality of love in its different varieties, and of sex, is thereby illuminated in ways that neither Kant nor Schopenhauer could properly imagine.

My criticism of Kant and Schopenhauer need not be thought to signify that *everything* in the cosmos should or can be treated with compassion, or as an end and not as merely a means. Vague though it may be, Nietzsche's idea of amor fati (love and acceptance of all reality) would seem to endorse that aspiration. It is, however, quite remote from the ethical sensibility that most people have had in the course of human development. Schopenhauer's outlook is more moderate insofar as it inhabits a conceptual niche somewhere between Kant's and Nietzsche's. The compassion that Schopenhauer defines as the basis of morality reaches out to the totality of animate existence, not to humankind only, but it plausibly refrains from extending itself to material nature as a whole.

For ecological reasons, we may feel that we have responsibilities to the physical environment, and this feeling may become a focus of our attitude toward everything that exists. Even so, that attitude is not directly moral, though it may be moral indirectly and to the degree that human interests, or those of life in general, are at stake. Belief in amor fati involves a further orientation, one that is metaphysical or religious in its cosmic scope. It requires a mode of thinking that goes beyond good and evil. But then, it may well exceed the limits of what members of our species can ever achieve, or even understand. For many of us this will always be an insurmountable hurdle.

3

Sexual Pluralism
and Its Limits

The pluralistic approach to sex tries to change attitudes that prevailed for at least twenty-five hundred years and have filtered down into the research of many contemporary scientists. Sexuality has been a subject of Western thought ever since Plato spoke about the universal drive called Eros that causes all creatures to seek for self-completion in relation to another member of their species. But the scientific study of sex is fairly recent in its origins. Some historians may find the beginnings of sexology in the writings of Krafft-Ebing and Havelock Ellis at the end of the nineteenth century; others go as far back as Leeuwenhoek in the seventeenth century, or even to Leonardo da Vinci in the fifteenth. In many ways, however, the science of sexology begins with the more theoretical generalizations about sexual behavior that Freud articulated in his *Three Essays on the Theory of Sexuality*, written in 1905 and revised in subsequent years.

In that book Freud incorporates the mainstream of medical presuppositions about sex, some of them originating with the Greeks. Not entirely, but to a large extent, current sexology has made the advances it can rightly claim by emancipating itself from the influence of both Freud and his predecessors. Freud himself lamented the fact that so little had been done to verify or falsify by empirical means the sexological generalizations that had been handed down from one authority to another. He wished to turn all speculation about such matters into purely scientific investigations. The possibility that psychoanalysis itself would someday become a science comparable to physics or chemistry underlay many of his own hypotheses.

Beginning with the successors to Freud, particularly those who criticized him for being too speculative, sexology tried to emulate the quantitative methodology of the well-established sciences. Sociologists like Kinsey approached sexual phenomena with the same concern for statistical accuracy that Kinsey himself had revealed in studying the behavior of gall wasps. And in the procedures of Masters and Johnson, human sexuality became a subject for laboratory research on a par with the work that many scientists were doing in their experiments with the physiology of reproduction among lower animals. Although the enterprise is still very recent, and frequently impeded by distrust toward anyone who seeks the truth in these areas, sexology may now take pride in being at least quasi-scientific.

But having freed itself from many vagaries of the past, sexology faces dangers that are characteristic of the life sciences. In attempting to be quantitative and precise, it runs the risk of becoming alienated from the human reality that the earlier tradition, rooted in literature and the humanism of classical studies, reflected as a matter of course. Whether they are being questioned by a sociologist or observed by a physiologist, people under study in a laboratory do not always reveal what is most important about themselves. And those who submit to observation are often unrepresentative of those who do not. Mainly intuitive as they may have been, the writings of poets, novelists, historians, and even speculative philosophers frequently described the varieties of human feeling with greater insight than is sometimes attained through scientific research.

Sexology may eventually succeed in combining the accuracy of science with this larger sensitivity to individual diversity which often appears in humanistic studies. We cannot hope to understand the nature and the values of sexuality if we limit ourselves to either of these approaches. Without the methods of scientific investigation, the humanities can founder in loose suppositions, which may easily degenerate into dogmatic beliefs showing none of that sensitivity to which I referred. Without the immersion in everyday experience that the humanities take as their native province, the life sciences lose their awareness of life in its immediacy and tend to blur the differences among human responses.

It is this kind of blurring that hampered the earlier stages in modern sexological theory. Both Freud and Masters and Johnson suffered from an essentialism that underlies most of their analyses. By essentialism I mean the assumption that in all sexological matters there must be a single, basic, uniform pattern prescribed by nature itself. In the case of Freud, this view derives from his doctrine of the libido, which I will be discussing in the following section. Masters and Johnson, too, believed in uniformities that serve as a normative underpinning for their therapeutic advice as well as their theorization about sexual response. Though Freud focused upon the differences between male and female, whereas Masters and Johnson emphasized the similarities, they both thought of sexuality as a unitary syndrome more or less alike in all human beings.

Masters and Johnson also resembled Freud in thinking that within this identity each of the sexes must have its own pattern of response: one for the male and one for the female. As a consequence, they employed essentialistic criteria for the normality and preferability of gender-related types of sexual behavior. To this extent, Masters and Johnson were traditionalists no less than Freud and the Freudians whom they criticized. Both camps showed the influences of a doctrinaire philosophy—its origins in Plato and Aristotle—that believed there must be a single structure to all sexuality and that it expresses itself in appropriate behavior of male or female.

Though this outlook is superseded by much that has happened in professional sexology during the last twenty-five years, it still lingers as an unexamined predilection on the part of many theorists. As against that essentialistic approach, I argue for a pluralistic outlook that William James continually recommended in his efforts to understand human life as a whole. He used his pluralism most effectively in *The Varieties of Religious Experience*, a book that virtually created the scientific study of religious phenomenology. At each point he denied that everything that might authentically be called a religious experience belonged to any one pattern or could be subsumed under a single model of explanation.

James also rejected the idea that all religious attitudes can be reduced to the sexual. In our age, sexual experience itself has sometimes acquired the importance that religion had at the time James was writing. One might even say that for many people in our day sexuality offers the only meaningful equivalent to religious ecstasy. It therefore becomes imperative that the study of sex should not be constrained by simplistic categories or essentialistic concepts of what is natural or normal or uniquely desirable.

By "pluralism" in this context I mean the refusal to presuppose that nature ordains one and only one structure for male and female sexual response, that there is any norm that can indicate how all men or women must behave as a means of functioning properly in sex, that there is a unique type of consummation that satisfies either male or female urges, that there is some particular instinct that constitutes or universally conditions sexual experience in everyone on every occasion, or that there is a unitary biological system fundamental in human sexuality.

In the first half of the twentieth century, the sexologist who best combined a scientific attitude with some appreciation of the pluralistic viewpoint was Kinsey. But even he often showed signs of essentialism, as in passages such as the following:

> Apparently many females, even though they may be slow to respond in coitus, may masturbate to orgasm in a matter of a minute or two. Masturbation thus appears to be a better test than coitus of the female's actual capacities; and there seems to be something in the coital technique which is responsible for her slower responses there.[1]

The first sentence in this quote states an empirical generalization that is undoubtedly true: many women achieve orgasm through masturbation more quickly than in coitus. From this, Kinsey concludes that masturbation seems to indicate "the female's actual capacities" better than coitus does. To say that, however, is to assume that orgasms are all alike and therefore that sexual ability can be measured regardless of how they are induced. It also assumes that a woman's aptitude in this respect can be gauged by the speed with which she reaches orgasm rather than the degree and quality of her sexual enjoyment or, in general, her emotional attunement with another person.

And finally, it assumes that there is something specifiable that tells us what a female may be capable of—not merely a summing up of empirical data about individual women, but also a revelation of what all women are like in their sexual being.

As a sexual pluralist, I suggest that this search for uniformity can be justified on neither scientific nor therapeutic grounds. People are different among themselves, each unique and irreducibly distinct though frequently similar to other members of the species. Within the great variety of their responses, we must also recognize that even inhibitions can have a salutary as well as unavoidable part to play. Not every instance of Victorian or puritanical restraint is harmful or "unnatural" or just a residue of childhood training. What is called repression is sometimes caused by innate tendencies that are as much an element of sexuality as liberated inclinations characterized by a lack of inhibitory control.

In treating inhibitions as components of human nature that may be as normal as any other, the pluralism I advocate owes much to the work of recent ethology, primatology, and behavioral biology as a whole. Investigators in those fields have described many instances in which animals are, as it were, "programmed" with inhibitory reactions that shield them from behavior detrimental to themselves or to their species. In the case of human beings, both sexual response and sexual inhibition are more complex. They are subject to subtler social influence and are less constant in their operation. They fade in and out in ways that are more erratic than for other animals.

Later in this chapter I will briefly sketch a pluralistic critique of Masters and Johnson, but the essentialism in Freud's doctrine of the libido is worth considering first. Those who criticize a great man, either overtly or indirectly, often duplicate some of his assumptions about the nature of their joint enterprise. It is the link that facilitates communication and thus enables the critics to develop a position of their own. This has happened in relation to Freud. By studying his essentialism, as well as a corresponding essentialism in critics like Masters and Johnson, we may be able to bolster some of the newer directions in sexology which can free us from these pioneering predecessors.

※

If Freud had been writing at the time of Plato, he would have called his idea of libido a poetic "myth." The libido myth suggests that the sexuality of human beings can be explained by reference to two separate coordinates: one is society or civilization, and that is highly variable; but the other is a fixed and determinate instinct, a source of energy ultimately alike in all human beings. This source of energy Freud called libido. Though he could not inspect it in isolation, he felt that it has to be posited as an innate force throughout sexual development. Since libido recognizes no goal for itself other than immediate satisfaction, it must be harnessed by the restraints imposed by society. Such controls insinuate themselves into the unconscious, but in principle they are external to libido as a separate entity. Society is repressive inherently, and so forever at war with the sexual instinct.

Why do I call this a myth? Surely we all realize that we have sexual impulses that society restrains; and in the polymorphous hedonism of infancy we may detect a freedom to enjoy organic pleasures which life in society eventually hampers. One might say that in infants libido shows itself forth, and that later developments manifest its vicissitudes within an alien dimension. This, however, is not Freud's argument. Libido as he envisages it cannot be fully perceived in the behavior of an infant or, for that matter, of anyone else. Libido is, for him, a hypothetical construct—something that pervades all human sexuality but can never be observed in itself. Furthermore, it changes inwardly as a person matures. From the polymorphous perverse condition of infancy, it moves through a series of transformations that culminate in what Freud calls normal genitality. At all stages in its progress, libido appears only in its interaction with society. Though it always remains hidden, it alone provides men and women with a sexual nature that social arrangements may then modify and redirect.

Freud's myth is fascinating, but if humanity does not possess "a nature"—a single, uniform, and universal state of being—it is quite misleading to say that people have a basic sexuality of the sort that Freud describes and are motivated by a libido that constitutes some innate program underlying their varied responses. That would mean that their sexual development has a fixed direction one could plot in advance of any person's experience. *Normal* development would hence involve growth or maturation that is determined by the powerful instinct itself.

We talk that way about processes such as walking or even speaking. It is as if our legs were "made" for walking. Children whose bone structure or bodily coordination prevents them from walking, instead of enabling them to do so, are deficient in a manner that we can recognize. If sexuality is similar, as Freud maintains, then it must lead to a process that is analogous in its organic being to a person's capacity to walk. He thought that for sexuality this process, the optimal expression of the relevant impulse, must be coital behavior serving the needs of reproduction. In its normal, that is, normative and not just frequent, employment the instinctual biology of sex had to eventuate in heterosexual coitus.

The sexuality of human beings would therefore consist in the successive stages of the libido, which change as an individual matures but always in the direction of a predetermined goal. Freud considered this process to be essentially the same as in the development "of a caterpillar into a butterfly." As he says: "The turning-point of this development is the subordination of all the component sexual instincts under the primacy of the genitals and along with this the subjection of sexuality to the reproductive function."[2] In other words, we become completely sexual, normal, and mature in the only way that applies to human nature, when we outgrow the caterpillar stage of libidinal development and orient our erotic or romantic interests toward the genital behavior of coitus.

On this view sexual perversions are responses that deflect libido from its natural progression. They freeze it into one or another of its preliminary stages. Neuroses do not arrest libido in this fashion, but they too interfere with its normal functioning. In neither perversion nor neurosis can libido reach the definitive consummation, the satisfying release of tension, established by the sheer genetic structure of every human organism.

This Freudian myth is not fanciful. Neither is it revolutionary in the history of ideas. It hews closely to what common sense has led most people to expect in life: on the one hand, sexual instinct that develops through involuntary maturation; on the other, civilization, morality, and spiritual transcendence that alter and restrict our instinctual urges. The dualism runs through all Western philosophy; and the Judeo-Christian tradition could hardly have existed without it. It is in fact a conventional, routine, and even moderate way for people to think about their sexuality.

Nevertheless, Freud's dualism is unacceptable. It is inaccurate in its interpretation of sexual behavior, and dangerous, even pernicious, in the moral mandates it helps to found. By identifying the sexual with the reproductive, it lends support to what Freud himself called "the tyranny of the genital." Freud continually recommended tolerance toward nongenital predilections, but his doctrine arrogates to libidinal interest a preferential status as that which is fundamental in all human sexuality. This would be justifiable if there were something in the nature of reproductive behavior which *defined* sexual response as such. But the empirical data do not suggest anything like that. Reproduction is but one of the ends of human sexuality, and only occasionally is it the principal one.

In setting libido apart from society or civilization, Freud wished to link human sexuality to the sexuality of lower organisms from which we have evolved. In most of the mammalian species, sexual behavior is automatic rather than deliberative, inherited rather than learned, genetically programmed rather than socially constructed. Rats who have been reared in total isolation copulate in ways that are indistinguishable from the behavior of rats who have been reared in their natural environment. But among primates the situation is much more complicated. Chimpanzees who have not seen the mating gestures of other chimpanzees will not perform sexually until they have spent a long period in the company of prospective mates. Harry F. Harlow's classic experiments with rhesus monkeys indicate that playing with peers during childhood may also be a necessary prelude to mature sexuality. Far from being instinctual in any pure and simple manner, coitus and even sexual desire seem to have a close connection with social experiences to which these primates had to be introduced. More recent studies confirm Harlow's findings.[3]

Once we get to human beings, cultural influences take on such importance that it becomes virtually impossible to separate sexual instinct from sexual learning. Freud and the Freudians admit this, indeed insist upon it. But for them the unity of sex and society merely means that the "overt manifestations" of the sexual instinct are culturally modified. Beneath all empirical appearances, libido is thought to keep on flowing in its own domain, though we see it only after it has been transfigured by society. If however, primates require interaction with the group in order to be capable of copulation, and if human beings have an even greater dependence upon learning and acculturation for the expression of their sexuality, why *should* we posit an unobservable libido that exists in separation from environmental factors? Is it not preferable to view our sexuality as having a highly intimate relationship with human society, to consider them inextricably intermeshed without postulating a hypothetical residue?

I advocate this approach as a more faithful representation of the fact that sexuality in our species is thoroughly conditioned by social and interpersonal needs as well as by physiological urgencies. A savage who somehow survived in a wilderness without associating with other people might well have the organic prerequisites for sex. In the case of a male, his genitals would grow, periodically fill with semen, and even discharge themselves through involuntary or masturbatory orgasm. But such experience would not be paradigmatic of human sexuality. That is characteristically a means of using our body to both communicate and bond with some other person, through one type of cathexis or another. In us, sex ordinarily occurs as a need for physical intimacy and interpersonal contact. Even in autoeroticism, it is as if one has become a second person to oneself. Sexual behavior depends upon bodily impulses at each particular moment, and so the state of organic maturation is always crucial; but it is only as a sociobiological phenomenon that sexuality in Homo sapiens can be understood at any level of its operation.

To reject the dualism between libido and society is also to recast the problem of repression. According to Freud, as well as thinkers like Herbert Marcuse and N. O. Brown, repression results from the reality principle throttling our drive for sexual pleasure. It is thought to be society, above all in Western civilization, damming up libido and preventing it from achieving satisfactions relevant to affective cravings in some individual. But if one cannot separate libido and society, as I am suggesting, this model for explaining the nature of repression must be rejected. As long as one doubts that there is a predetermined libido invested by nature itself, one cannot assert that sexuality need only liberate itself from social imposition in order to achieve its appointed consummations. Moreover we may possibly conclude that repression emanates from restraints within sexuality as well as those from the outside; and if these inner controls cannot be eliminated without damaging one's sexual response, we may have to reconsider the desirability of trying to eradicate repressiveness.

At the very least, our ideas about repression will have to be reformulated. Freud seemed to recognize this necessity in one or two places. In *Civilization and Its Discontents* he ends a chapter with these tantalizing words: "Sometimes one seems to perceive that it is not only the pressure of civilization but something in the nature of the [sexual] function itself which denies us full satisfaction and urges us along other paths. This may be wrong; it is hard to decide."[4] In a long footnote he then speculates about the possibility of there being an "organic repression" that evolved along with the growth of civilization. This organic or innate repression he interprets as a defense against animal sexuality. Freud thinks it may have arisen in early human beings when they assumed the erect gait and began to depreciate the sense of smell.

In the second of his three "Contributions to the Psychology of Love," Freud offers another reason why the native being of sexuality precludes absolute gratification. He remarks that "at its beginning sexual instinct is divided into a large number of components—or, rather, it develops from them—not all of which can be carried on into its final form; some have to be suppressed or turned to other uses before the final form results."[5] As an example of these suppressed components, Freud cites sadistic elements that belong to the instinct but must be "abandoned." But if libido develops by suppressing these components, one might have concluded that organic repression *enables* the final form of human sexuality to achieve its appropriate satisfaction. Although elements like the sadistic may sometimes be denied gratification, the sexual experience that results from such repression may be wholly satisfying in view of what the human organism is at that time. And if there can be no one "final form," as I maintain, neither can we say which among the alternate responses must or should or will be abandoned in every case.

If this is true, the problem of repression would seem to be more difficult than even Freud had imagined; and perhaps that is why he terminates the discussion by ritualistically repeating his cardinal belief in libido as a single, basic, unitary force: "All such developmental processes, however, relate only to the upper layers of the complicated structure. The fundamental processes which promote erotic impulse remain always the same."[6]

❊

In questioning the essentialism of Freud, we need not eliminate words like *libidinal* from the English language. The adjectival form is useful as a demarcation of one type of sexuality, provided we realize that it does not refer to an exclusive something that is *the* sexual instinct or sexuality in its essence. And once we discard the essentialistic conception, we may find that sex often involves its own constraints while civilization can be liberating as well as repressive.[7] In the need for privacy, and in general the need to inhibit sexual response in some respect, we may detect the concrete implications of what Freud called organic repression. But the barriers may also have issued from social, as well as biological, factors that *further* human sexuality instead of merely curtailing it.

Freud's ideas about organic repression have not had much effect on contemporary sexology. But the belief in a unified substratum continues in more recent theorists, whether or not they received it directly from Freud. Behavioral scientists usually do not concern themselves with the libido per se. Kinsey does not list it in his index; and in their glossary, Masters and Johnson define it simply as "sexual drive or urge."[8] Even so, they and many of the recent researchers who have been influenced by them tend to insist upon an all-pervading identity of physiological response, not only in male and female human beings but also in all other mammals.

Kinsey begins by saying that the variations in sexual response "offer endless possibilities for combination and recombination," but then he immediately qualifies this by assertions about "basic" patterns: "Consequently the responses of each individual may be quite unlike those of any other individual, although the basic physiologic patterns of sexual response and orgasm are remarkably uniform among all individuals, both female and male, and throughout all of the species of mammals."[9] At times, Kinsey did sound as if he thought there are many different patterns, all equally basic, but in his summary and conclusions he flatly states that "orgasm is a phenomenon which appears to be essentially the same in the human female and male."[10] On the next page he admits that this is somewhat surprising since in every other mammalian species orgasm occurs only infrequently among the females. He does not perceive that this generalization contradicts what he has just been saying about the remarkable uniformity among all individuals in all species of mammals.

In Masters and Johnson, the belief in a physiologic uniformity that accompanies the variety of sexual behavior recurs throughout their theory as well as their therapy. They think of the male as following a standard mode of ejaculatory reaction, and they do not acknowledge any major differences within the characteristics of the female orgasm apart from duration and intensity. Although they provide three models for the female sexual response cycle, one of these is considered nonorgasmic and another is simply a reiteration that occurs in multiple orgasmic response. In its main attributes the orgasm is taken to be the same for all women as it is for all men.

Masters and Johnson are sometimes confusing about this, since they often admit the existence of diversity even when they are arguing for uniformity. Speaking of quantitative and qualitative elements in the female orgasm, they say that these are "totally variable between one woman's orgasmic experiences, and orgasm as it occurs in other women." But in the very next sentence they assert that "baseline physiologic reactions . . . remain consistent from orgasm to orgasm."[11] They repeatedly state that "basic orgasmic physiology" is the same for all variations both in the types of stimulation and in the individual responsiveness that different women experience. Obviously, the words "baseline" and "basic" are important here. Whatever else they mean, these terms bespeak a uniform structure despite the recurrent evidences of diversity.

Why should we believe in this fundamental uniformity? In discussing their method of approach, Masters and Johnson list two questions that guided their research: "What physical reactions develop as the human male and female respond to effective sexual stimulation? Why do men and women behave as they do when responding to effective sexual stimulation?"[12] Throughout their writing, the phrase "effective sexual stimulation" occurs time and time again. It contains within it the core of Masters and Johnson's essentialism. Their investigation is always directed toward selected modes of response, and only behavior that leads to these is considered "effective sexual stimulation." No other behavior, however characteristic or satisfying it may be, is taken to be definitive of the sexual cycle. To say then that the physiology of male or female orgasm is basically the same can only manifest the consequences of limiting oneself to a single pattern for both genders. Everything else having been eliminated from a previously established category of *effective* stimulation, diversity in the basic physiology has been ruled out beforehand. And since this preferential system of biologic response defines the very nature of human sexuality as Masters and Johnson see it, we are back to a nonverifiable faith not too dissimilar from Freud's belief in an underlying libido.

The consequences of holding this faith are evident at several places in Masters and Johnson's work. It affects the choice of study-subjects whom they accepted in their research population, and it slants the conclusions they garnered from their observations. They themselves list several criteria for admission which created "selectivity" in the research population. The most pertinent of these criteria is what they call "facility of sexual responsiveness."[13] That means that the subjects under observation would have to be men or women whose sexual performance matched the prior conditions incorporated in the notion of effective stimulation.

Though Masters and Johnson were working with a "small, arbitrarily selected segment of male and female society" (as they freely confess), their general conclusions were inevitably molded by what they assumed that human sexuality *must* be like: "Attempts to answer the challenge inherent in the question, 'What do men and women do in response to effective sexual stimulation?' have emphasized the *similarities, not the differences* in the anatomy and physiology of human sexual response."[14] In saying this, Masters and Johnson are extrapolating from their sample, in which the similarities may very well have been more noteworthy than the differences. But if one is to make statements about human sexuality in general, one must also emphasize significant differences that Masters and Johnson neglected or minimized because they did not see them.

To describe and analyze the sexological data with utmost fidelity is to recognize that there can be no justification for either Freud's essentialism or Masters and Johnson's. We need only to delineate different kinds of response that present themselves to careful observation. We might also make therapeutic recommendations, but they would not be the same for all people on all occasions. The pluralistic attitude I am advocating employs this approach as a corrective to the falsifications and the biases that essentialism frequently creates.

❄

The pluralistic approach can be of help for resolving various problems about human sexuality, but possibly those about the orgasm most of all. Though men and women cherish other elements in their sexual experience, the orgasm serves as an obvious state of sexual fulfillment. It is a consummation that reveals much of what we mean by sexual goodness. We must ask ourselves, however, the following questions: Is the orgasm a single entity or a diverse class of responses referred to by a single word; is it similar for male and female; is it the most important consummation in sex; and is it or is it not the goal for all sexual experience that people have considered successful and richly satisfying? We must also ask ourselves what is the relationship between the orgasm and what is called "sexual relief" or "release of sexual tension."

Built into this questioning is the concept of organic striving that can possibly result in an agreeable and life-enhancing resolution. Kinsey speaks of "a quiescence, a calm, a peace, a satisfaction with the world which, in the minds of many persons, is the most notable aspect of any type of sexual activity."[15] He employs these words to describe the postorgasmic state, but we may wonder whether they are true of all orgasms, and whether they are true of no sexual responses other than the orgasm.

Both before and after Masters and Johnson began their experimental studies, sexologists have attested to the ambiguity in what people call an orgasm. To define it as "the peak of sexual excitement during sexual activity" (a definition that one often sees) is of no use, since we do not know what kind of peak truly matters.[16] Furthermore, ideas of consummation or sexual discharge involve physiological as well as psychological coordinates.

We usually assume that satisfaction will be something physical while also being something that is felt. But determining the relationship between the physiological and the psychological is a difficult problem, for scientists as well as philosophers. And in relation to the orgasm, one often encounters situations in which physiological and psychological criteria seem to conflict. Some women show a physiological reaction characteristic of the orgasm but claim to be sexually unsatisfied; others report total satisfaction although their behavioral responses would have led many physiologists to deny that they could be having an orgasm. If we admit all the variations, we run a risk of allowing too much into our conception of sexual release. But if we exclude or too greatly downplay the diversity among individual consummations, we return to the essentialism we are trying to escape.

Thus pluralism is fraught with difficulties in itself. It cannot be automatic in its application, and it must accept the fact that it, too, has limitations. These are troublesome with regard to the morality of sex as well as to the study of what its nature is. I turn now to both of these problems.

❅

By approaching human sexuality from a pluralistic point of view, we avoid the temptation to think that all people are essentially alike. With this in mind, we may go on to formulate sophisticated hypotheses about different types of sexual response that matter to men and women. These differences have ramifications throughout our lives, morally as well as sexologically. Moreover, the pluralistic approach provides a framework for my claim that sex, love, and compassion are internally related; and also for my distinction between the sensuous and the passionate.

In discussing the latter, I tried to show how they may function together harmoniously throughout the great variability in each. The sensuous appears in our search for sensory gratification, the passionate in the goodness of emotional fulfillment. I denied that either is necessarily preferable to the other, or inherently incompatible with it. The same applies to relations between sex, love, and compassion.[17] Even if this line of reasoning is useful, however, I must admit that some of the most interesting questions about human sexuality still remain unanswered. They may even seem as irresolvable as before.

For instance, I originally lamented the mere existence of conflicts between the sensuous and the passionate, but even at this late date I am unable to provide a blueprint for eliminating those conflicts. Harmonization between the two modes of sexuality is probably unavailable to many people on most occasions. And even when it is available, it may not always be preferable to the satisfactions that accrue without harmonization. Describing psychological and physiological correlates of harmonization is not the same as determining how it can actually be achieved—or when it should be. In my pluralistic manner, have I only been analyzing possibilities for enjoyment while letting others decide what is best?

That is not entirely true, for I have also defended a series of viable potentialities from which people may choose as they wish. And if we portray these human opportunities with clarity and sympathetic corroboration, do we not make them more significant for those who might otherwise ignore their ingredient consummations, or fail to maximize their accessibility?

Even so, the initial questions may seem to be no less vexatious than they always were. Faced with the disparate but equally authentic responses that pluralism recognizes, my readers may not feel that this greater understanding enables them to have the better sexual lives that they desire. Of course, they may not feel any need to change. Some people will continue to prefer the sensuous or the passionate to the exclusion of the other; and some will seek to harmonize them occasionally but not often, or at different times and in different ways. It is always possible that such choices may be unfortunate, however, and I am not confident that what I have said thus far provides the assistance that people may require in order to make suitable decisions.

We cannot avoid these drawbacks by saying that the philosophy of sex is different from counseling or giving practical advice. Our generalizations in one field always affect our conclusions in the other. In this regard, consider Mary Jane Sherfey's assertion that the number of orgasms attained by a woman is "a measure of the human female's orgasmic potentiality."[18] This purely numerical criterion is related to what that theorist considered females to be in their very essence. Presupposing a basic insatiability in all women, Sherfey inferred that only civilization impedes free and unlimited sexual activity:

> Having no cultural restrictions, these [infrahuman] primate females will perform coitus from twenty to fifty times a day during the peak week of estrus, usually with several series of copulations in rapid succession. If necessary, they flirt, solicit, present, and stimulate the male in order to obtain successive coitions. They will "consort" with one male for several days until he is exhausted, then take up with another. They emerge from estrus totally exhausted, often with wounds from spent males who have repulsed them. I suggest that something akin to this behavior could be paralleled by the human female if her civilization allowed it.[19]

Whatever one may think about this theory of human nature, it must be seen in its contrast with the opposite but equally extreme ideas about female sexuality that were present in the thinking of an old-line Freudian like Marie

Bonaparte. Starting with the claim that only the "vaginal" type of woman is best adapted to the sexual function, and that this kind of woman has no need for sensuous foreplay or multiple orgasms, or anything else that departs from the reproductive aspects of coitus, Bonaparte had a different conception of the female. She saw her as innately a monogamous and socially passive person who defines herself in terms of home and children. Though it prevailed in Western civilization for many centuries, this model is disappearing very rapidly. How it can be replaced by new ideals, new modes of life that will allow women to fulfill themselves in accordance with their own individual inclinations, remains as a problem for us all.

Other problems, too, require further study. People in the Western world have created an idea of "perversion." The notion gave them the sustenance that comes from thinking there must be a right way and a wrong way in all matters of human behavior. Perversion was defined as the wrong way in sexuality. It was conceived to be "unnatural," "immature," "less than ideal" in view of what people are inherently.

If there is no human sexuality of a unitary sort, however, no univocal sexual instinct, no universal goal or requisite culmination, what can warrant this concept of perversion? Sexual failure is always possible; but as sexuality may succeed in any number of responses, nothing that works on those occasions can necessarily pervert it. But do we want to say that the so-called perversions are just alternative attitudes, each as valid as any other sexual possibility? Some may be incapable of yielding sexual satisfaction to anyone. And not infrequently they involve harm to other human beings, and are therefore morally wrong. Even if the pejorative essentialism has been removed, are we not confronted still by pervasive problems about value and about choice?

This kind of issue appears most glaringly in the question of homosexuality. Freud could not reach an unambiguous conclusion about it. In his famous letter to the mother of a homosexual, he says that her son does not require treatment and should not be considered neurotic simply because his libidinal interests are directed toward members of his own gender. In articles such as "'Civilized' Sexual Morality and Modern Nervous Illness," Freud attacked Western civilization for the cruelty and stupidity with which it has tyrannized over sexual minorities.[20] And yet, Freud constantly affirmed that libido has only one normal and natural goal: heterosexual coitus. In a remarkable sentence in the letter, the ambivalence or total confusion of his attitude reveals itself with astounding naiveté: "Homosexuality is assuredly no advantage but it cannot be classified as an illness; it is nothing to be ashamed of, no vice, no degradation, we consider it to be a variation of the sexual function produced by a certain arrest of sexual development."[21]

In speaking of homosexuality as "a variation of the sexual function," Freud would seem to be treating it as one of the devices by which the sexual instinct normally fulfills itself. But obviously that cannot be what he really means, since he immediately ascribes this variation to an arrested development of sexuality. The homosexual son was not to be classified as ill, but nevertheless his perversion could only be considered a condition that manifests persistent (and presumably undesirable) immaturity.

Neither of these two views in Freud is worthy of our credence. The latter is just a restatement of his essentialism, and the former would seem to be an ad hoc compensation for the bigotry that the myth of libido contains within itself. Freud did not go far enough in his condemnation of society's sexual intolerance. This fact of civilized existence is largely the consequence of assumptions, which the Freudian doctrine fosters as much as any other, that nature yields only one ideal direction for human sexuality, and that all who fail to live up to it must be inferior.

By rejecting essentialism, I am able to reject the idea that heterosexual coitus is or should be the sexual goal for all human beings. But from this I do not conclude that homosexual behavior is just another means—entirely comparable to heterosexuality in this respect—that anyone may indiscriminately use to express his or her inclinations. That is what some gay liberationists maintain in their struggle for absolute tolerance. The struggle is justified, but this reasoning seems no more warranted than the heterosexual prejudice it wishes to condemn. As usually formulated, the homosexual argument assumes that orgasms are all alike, that "the" sexual instinct is equally satisfied by every kind of orgasm, and therefore that an acceptable partner for any individual on any occasion can belong to either sex. As an instinctual activity, sex is thought to be in principle the same whether the beloved is male or female.

I am convinced that this belief is mistaken. What is appropriate or inappropriate, desirable or undesirable, in the choice of a sexual object will depend upon many variables, including one's physiological disposition, hormonal tendency, psychological development, personal experience, and social conditioning. As long as homosexuality remains a minority orientation in human beings, as in other species, it cannot function as an equivalent alternative by which everyone may express his or her sexuality. It must exist in a world that willy-nilly favors the sexual interests of the majority by cultivating them in many facets of daily life, by nurturing them in childhood, and by glamorizing them at maturity. This would happen even in utopia. It is unjust for society to increase whatever gay men or women may suffer as a result, and we should strive to extirpate anything that deprives them of their rights. But the fact remains that while some people may achieve their greatest satisfaction through homosexuality, it is likely that most others will not and never can.

We may and should create a world that becomes more sensitively responsive to the differences in sexual orientation, and we may encourage men and women to find satisfaction through any behavior of their choice that is not injurious to others; but we cannot enunciate general principles that would authoritatively indicate which kind of sex life is most suitable for all human beings. To do that we would need to have at hand sexological knowledge of a type that no science can yield as yet. We would need answers to questions about each individual's innately biological makeup, psychological maturation, experience in his or her society, and general capacity for attaining fulfillment through one or another sexual possibility. Given the scarcity of reliable data, we can only offer tentative suggestions in relation to the empirical and theoretical questions. And beyond them lurk ethical problems that may also make us wonder how much even a highly refined pluralism can achieve.

❄

These problems are worth considering at greater length. In asserting that we should encourage people to find sexual satisfaction through any behavior they choose, provided it does not harm others, what kind of statement was I making? And how can we know what will or will not be harmful? My exhortation was a moral, not a sexological or merely prudential, utterance. I was promoting an ideal that encompasses the widest range of sexual freedom compatible with our obligation to avoid hurting others, or violating their rights, regardless of what we ourselves might want. But though this principle combines sexual pluralism with a supervening concern about the welfare of those who might suffer from it, my recommendation was vague and largely unspecified.

Much of this indeterminacy results from the very nature of human sexuality. None of the criteria by which we might judge what is good or bad in sex can be shown to be objectively superior for all people in all situations. From this, it follows that the relative values of different kinds of sex are incommensurate as far as their inherent desirability is concerned. One could hold, for instance, that less pleasure is sometimes better than more, if the lesser pleasure is what someone who is involved prefers for any reason. All such adjudications would have to be made by each person only.[22]

But in addressing the moral implications of sex, we need valid standards of how we should or should not behave. As I claimed in the previous chapters of this book, neither the Kantian nor the Schopenhauerian approach to sexuality can provide them. For that matter, neither can the utilitarianism of John Stuart Mill and his followers help us very much. Though an enlightened society may be committed to promoting the greatest happiness of the greatest number, it would still have to determine what its attitude toward sexual diversity should be.

It is not enough for us to say, as most pluralists might, that there are many acceptable modes of sexual gratification and all adults should be allowed to choose what is best for themselves. We also need to know how children are to be educated in ways that will enable them to grow into sexual maturity, and how they should be encouraged to find their own fulfillment without making mistakes that will harm them as well as others.

One might answer that all this applies equally well to education of any kind. But the problems in sexuality are special, and uniquely challenging, if only because they first appear at a time in a young person's life when few of us are capable of handling the emotional strain they impose. Adolescence is a period of turbulence that awakens boys and girls to both the ecstasy and the potential painfulness of sexual exploration. Many who pass through this stage of human development do not find their way to any happy solution. Parental or other authorities may blandly intone the wisdom of the Buddha when he asserts, on virtually all occasions: "Work out your salvation with diligence." But that may not be sufficient under these circumstances.

The sexual education of children is designed to produce self-sustaining grownups who will routinely act in an ethical fashion while also enjoying the consummations of living in nature and society. But will this ideal facilitate our knowing whether obscenity and pornography, as these words are ordinarily used, should be banned or treated as free expression that no authority can rightly prohibit? If we choose toleration in sexual matters, should that be limited to activities that are totally nonviolent and include only consenting adults? And even if the courts decide that discrimination on the basis of sexual orientation is illegal, are parents wrong in trying to protect their children from the social stigma of being deviant?

Apart from the condemnation of extreme violence and the abuse of minors, agreement in these moral issues will always be hard to reach. The United States Supreme Court has ruled that in questions about obscenity and pornography the "local mores" of each community can serve as a general rule of thumb. But that might allow a majority of public opinion to tyrannize over the sexual preferences of some minority, and even to disregard interests that may be prevalent in a particular place and do no harm to anyone.

One could reply that people cut the Gordian knot by deciding as best they can about what is or is not ethical, or legal, or politically feasible in each case. But apart from taking note of how these sexual conundrums diversely emerge and are differently handled within their historical context, we might find little that we can justifiably recommend as pluralists. Though sexual pluralism teaches us to be as flexible as possible, the mere fact that it has limitations must always remind us that by itself it cannot settle the very problems that require it most of all.

4

The History of Love

Guest: Irving Singer
Interviewer: Robert Fulford

FULFORD: One of the fascinating ideas that emerges from your work is the difference between love as feeling and, on the other hand, ideas about love. And I think you've made the point that the feeling of love is universal among human beings, whereas ideas of love are extremely particular to a culture or historic period.

SINGER: Well, I modify that in emphasizing attitudes of love rather than feelings, since people are often capable of love and experience love without having any one feeling such that they can say "Ah, that is the feeling of love." And something comparable must be true of other species. Love is related to biological forces—what used to be called instincts—running throughout the mammalian species and possibly other creatures, too. The way they respond to their instincts, the way they use them, the way they interpret them (which human beings do constantly), the way people in different eras build systems of thought and religion—that varies tremendously.

FULFORD: Today, a major issue when you hear people talking about love, as opposed to writing about it, when they speak about it among themselves, a major issue seems to be a conflict between commitment on the one hand and passion, immediate passion on the other hand. I think that's something really that is there in the literature going a long way back.

SINGER: Yes, I think it does, and the conflict you mention was especially important in the twentieth century. There's a book by Bertrand Russell, *Marriage and Morals*, in which he addresses himself to this question in a very interesting way. He advocates romantic passion, and even says that anyone who's never experienced it has missed out on a great deal that's important in life. But once one gets married, he insists, one has to devote oneself to the children and to the family situation, and romantic passion no longer has any place. This represents a split between passion and commitment that I consider unfortunate and generally unwholesome. The big problem for philosophy and for behavior in our age consists in trying to find some means of overcoming that split in such a way that romantic passion is amenable to commitment, which by and large means marriage, and marriage or other long-term affiliations can incorporate something like the romantic passion with which a relationship may have begun.

FULFORD: Whenever someone like Russell becomes articulate about love and his or her experience of it, the idea of transcendence comes in here. The idea that when you are in love, when you have felt this thing that we've been feeling for thousands of years, and we all think about differently, when you feel this thing you become something greater than you were. There's a wonderful passage in Pasternak's *Doctor Zhivago*, where he says when we were expressing our love, Lara and I, physically but also far beyond physically, I felt that we were with all history and, indeed, with the gods and so on. It's a beautifully phrased expression of what many people feel. But where does that idea come from? Where do we start noting it in the history of our civilization?

SINGER: It's a great idea and it begins with Plato, who is possibly the greatest philosopher in the Western world. In Plato, you get the idea that love is an instinctual means by which human beings transcend their limitations in time and space. Christianity picked that up and interpreted the transcendence in terms of religious concepts of a divinity who was himself outside of time and space. But in later traditions, as in medieval courtly love and in Romantic love of the nineteenth century, you get a kind of naturalization or even humanization of love inasmuch as it need not be elicited by an ultimate Platonic form, or the Christian God, but rather issues from the mere experience of oneness between human beings on earth. Love as transcendence beyond this world is a magnificent idea. Unfortunately, it's wrong.

FULFORD: It's wrong even though Plato held it and many others repeated it?

SINGER: Yes.

FULFORD: Now, when you say wrong, why do you believe it's wrong? Transcendence, I mean, many people think they've had this experience.

SINGER: I'm a critic of that tradition, though I recognize its great importance and derive many of my own ideas from it, because it falsifies the way in which love is related to normal responses that belong to us as parts of nature rather than as entities that escape or reach beyond nature. Love has to be understood in terms of what happens to ordinary men and women in their ordinary relationships throughout their lives and in terms of the world that they live in. There's something in the *achievement*, something in the grandeur of having attained a relationship of love, that may be called "transcendent" in the sense of being wonderfully desirable and a consummation, but love does not take us into some transcendental realm apart from our natural state. Once you think that way, it becomes very hard to see how mere mortals like us are able to experience love.

FULFORD: So it's part of your philosophic project to really destroy the idea that we transcend ourselves mainly in love. You want to bring love down to being part of our worldly concern.

SINGER: Yes. That's exactly what I wish to do. I believe that the old tradition that thinks of love as transcending ordinary life neglects the way in which we belong to what George Santayana called the realm of matter. We arise from and live in a material order, and we are governed to a large extent by our physiological as well as our psychological determinants. If we're going to make sense of how ordinary people love each other, then we can't define love as being transcendent of the ordinary world they live in. When love succeeds, it is a transcendent good but there is no transcendental object that necessarily defines its being. The relationship of love is something that people, men and women, establish in their day-by-day experience with each other—assuming they have learned how to do so.

FULFORD: You mentioned that the idea of transcendence goes back to Plato. And, of course, the Greeks began many of our concepts of love, our ways of thinking about love. For them it was really an elite preoccupation, wasn't it? Almost a preoccupation of philosophers or people who defined themselves as philosophers.

SINGER: Elitist in various ways. The most interesting ideas about love in the Greek world are homosexual ideas that presuppose that love involves a kind of intellectual friendship only men can have with one another. Certainly that is an attitude we have long since outgrown. We foresee now the possibility of friendship between men and women that will allow them to obtain the kind of heightened love relationships that the Greeks were seeking. Their attitude was also elitist insofar as the philosophers were supposed to have a special faculty that enabled them to make that transcendental leap we were just talking about. If one no longer defines love in this way, there is no reason why ordinary people can't love as well as the Platonic philosophers. In the history of ideas, courtly and Romantic concepts have, in effect, been a kind of democratization of Greek thinking about love. They encouraged the belief that everybody can possibly attain a love worth having.

FULFORD: Democratization, first of all, in bringing in half of the human race. Because in the Greek concept, as you say, it was basically a male-to-male concept.

SINGER: Right.

FULFORD: That's where the real love of that kind could exist. And women were sort of a side issue, weren't they?

SINGER: They were not treated seriously. Certainly they were not treated as people who are capable of love. Aristotle even wonders whether women are persons—whether they are metaphysically the equal of men—that is, in their souls—and whether they have a humanity equal to what men have. We believe that he was obviously wrong. Our great challenge nowadays, when women are achieving equality in so many areas of life, is to see what kind of love is available to them as well as to men in the present world.

FULFORD: Among the Greeks, as they thought about it they must've noticed that they—many of the men—felt passion for women—enough passion to have children. But that man-woman passion was not, in their way of thinking, to be elevated into anything really exceptional or magical or anything like that.

SINGER: Right. It was not to be dignified.

FULFORD: Not to be dignified.

SINGER: Or given ideal status. Love is, and always has been, a great ideal in the Western world, and the idea that the passions of ordinary men and women could be dignified as love was very threatening to the Greeks. In a sense, the Judeo-Christian tradition introduces this possibility since every person, every child of God, could hope to aspire toward the love of God. But in that tradition there wasn't a full realization that in their natural state men and women could have an authentic love independent of the love of God. In the Middle Ages the church's ideas about marriage, for instance, were very wholesome inasmuch as it was treated as a sacramental bonding of male and female. But that was only because marriage was considered a partnership within the community of people seeking God. The church failed to see that men and women, in or out of marriage, can achieve a kind of natural love that may be equal to the love of God, and even independent of it.

FULFORD: The courtly, really medieval, conception was partly based on Christianity, partly looked back to the Greeks, but developed something of its own.

SINGER: Right. There you find the process of democratization beginning. The ideas in courtly love are sometimes Christian, and sometimes Neoplatonic, except that it is the relationship between men and women that now becomes the focal point.

Very special men and women. The man would be a great hero, particularly a military hero; the woman would be the most beautiful female around. They would both be . . .

FULFORD: Of noble birth.

SINGER: Often of the highest birth. Queens, princes, princesses. They would be exceptional examples of what men and women can become. But they were men and women in nature, and that made a very big difference. That was the beginning of this process of extending the ideal of love to ordinary people.

FULFORD: But it was a very special and exceptional kind of love that the courtly troubadors sang of, in Provence and such places. They sang of a very special kind of love, self-sacrificial, of course, and something very, very much beyond what we think of as ordinary, everyday love.

SINGER: In a sense, yes. Still it wasn't special in the way that some scholars have thought. There's a scholarly view, I'm sure you know, that thinks of courtly love as being based on frustration, self-abnegation, denial of one's talents and capacities; and there was a segment within courtly love that took that attitude. But there are other varieties of courtly love in which the satisfaction of one's instinctual needs is very much recognized and accepted. It's just that since the men and women were so outstanding they were expected to show their love in elevated and extraordinary ways. Courtly or Romantic love was generally very ethical, highly idealistic, concerned about great achievements of the spirit that men and women could experience in their relationship with each other. Only that could prove they really had a bond of love. The warrior would have to go out and do heroic deeds, and the woman would have to be the faithful beloved who waits for her lover to return from his glorious enterprises.

FULFORD: And she would be the inspiration of the warrior, too. He would fight for her, fight to glorify her.

SINGER: Right. But he was also fighting for the right to attain her. He was fighting for the ability to have a reciprocal relationship. He wasn't fighting merely to be frustrated by her.

FULFORD: Right. But to deserve her also.

SINGER: To deserve her love. Precisely.

FULFORD: But in that context, I think, the tragedy of love was born. Is that fair to say? That is, the idea that you could have a doomed love and it would still be extremely beautiful.

SINGER: It's doomed and it's tragic because the world doesn't understand it. I think that's the message of courtly love. The medieval world recognized the importance of marriage. But it was not the same as love. Marriages were primarily economic or political arrangements. They could include sexual love between the spouses but often didn't.

FULFORD: Certainly in the class we're speaking of, which is the nobles and the royals and so on.

SINGER: So if there were a love relationship of the sort that courtly love advocated, that might have to occur outside marriage, and therefore, to a large extent, outside the social order. The tragedy arises when love and marriage come into conflict. The legend of Tristan and Iseult in the Middle Ages portrays what happens when the two are separated and do come into conflict with each other. The woman and the man suffer terribly despite their heroic attempt to accept and harmonize the values of both marriage and love.

FULFORD: The possibility that is in the medieval and the Renaissance period of dying for love—Romeo and Juliet in

Shakespeare most famously—and it being somehow admirable and beautiful—that was a product of that age, wasn't it?

SINGER: Right. But remember, it's not very much different from the idea of dying for any other ideal. Many persons have died for love of country. Many persons have died for reasons of religion. Human beings are programmed, I think, to construct ideals that then become so important that people are prepared to die for them. Love is a supreme example of something that individuals have either died for, or felt they'd be willing to die for, because it is such a powerful ideal. And that's part of the meaning, I think, of courtly ideas about love: that the men and women involved are so greatly dedicated to love that their life no longer matters to them once they realize they cannot fulfill this ideal here on earth.

FULFORD: The love is greater than everything else, including their life.

SINGER: Not that they want to die, but they are ready to do so if they have to choose between life and love.

FULFORD: The ideal, the central idea on which mass communications, mass fiction are based today, is Romantic love. A couple of hundred years ago this ideal grew up and filled literature and so on. Where did that Romantic idea of love come from?

SINGER: Well, in part it came from the Platonic origin, from the Christian context, and from the desire to humanize and democratize Platonic and Christian ideas through courtly love. And then there was the reaction against courtly love, which took place in the sixteenth and seventeenth and beginning of the eighteenth centuries, when people felt that courtly love was just too elevated and unrealistic. It was in fact too far from what ordinary human beings actually experienced. As a result, a split occurred during the period represented by rationalist philosophy on the Continent—mainly in the seventeenth and early eighteenth centuries—a split between the conditions needed for people to live together well, in an orderly marriage for instance, and the conditions demanded by courtly love, or in general idealized sexual love of any sort. There was a great skepticism on the part of Montaigne, Descartes, and many others about the ability to harmonize married love with sexual love. The idea of Romantic love arose as a reaction against that.

FULFORD: A reaction against that separation of the two things.

SINGER: Yes, it was a reaction against the skeptical attitude of the previous century.

FULFORD: Right.

SINGER: History often runs in terms of action and reaction and, in this case, the concept of Romantic love was an attempt by people in the nineteenth century to respond to the cynicism of their predecessors in the seventeenth and eighteenth centuries. In doing so, they returned to courtly love, Neoplatonic love, Christian love . . .

FULFORD: And combined them all. And they were really saying to their grandfathers or their great-grandfathers of the enlightenment of the seventeenth and early eighteenth centuries: We want to put aside your coolness, your rationality, your skepticism. We want to commit ourselves in our poetry, our thinking, our feeling, to this whole full-bodied love of man and woman.

SINGER: Right. And such love was more accessible to large numbers of people in the nineteenth century because of industrialization that had brought a relative degree of wealth to Europe. Social customs had changed—families and parents didn't have the power to choose who would marry whom to the extent that they had previously. Individuals could carve out their own destiny. And when individuals do that, they generally want to marry somebody they can love. Romantic love provided an intellectual framework in which one could justify and explain erotic choices that young men and women were now making, partly on the basis of sexual preferences but also on the basis of idealizations that transmute such preferences into a special and honorific kind of attachment.

FULFORD: So the new economy of the industrial age was providing opportunities for people to leave home and set up their own lives.

SINGER: Right.

FULFORD: And Romantic love, through the poetry and fiction of the day, was there to say you should direct your feelings this way: fasten them on this one man, this one woman, and that will be your deepest, fullest commitment.

SINGER: Moreover, with some hope of success. At the beginning of the tradition of Romantic love there was an enormous amount of optimism. This was related to the French Revolution and to the feelings millions of people had in Europe that now we are creating a new world; we have erased the old order; the old regimes are crumbling throughout each of the countries in Europe; we can have all sorts of democratic possibilities, one of which involves the freedom to choose someone in accordance with our own taste, and to do so with the justification of living up to this ideal that has evolved in Western thought over a period of centuries. It was a time of great hope, great enthusiasm, great buoyancy. Romantic poetry and philosophy lent themselves to all this very readily.

FULFORD: And that was really a flowering of an idea that had been there all along. Now there was a chance to play it out.

SINGER: It had been there but submerged, not fully developed, not extended to the large numbers in the population that may previously have felt inclinations to love.

FULFORD: I realize it was expressed in a thousand or ten thousand ways, but how would you sum up that ideal of Romantic love?

SINGER: Well, one way of doing that is to think of it in relation to Christian ideas about love. In Christianity there is a transcendental entity, God, who is outside of time and space, and love consists either in his bestowing goodness upon the world for no reason other than this being what belongs to his nature—in Christianity God *is* love—or else love is creation searching to respond to God's love, to return it reciprocally to him. As a result of all sorts of things that were happening in theology and in philosophy, Romantic love reverses the slogan "God is love" and says that love is God, that wherever you find love you are experiencing God. Once you make that shift, it's no longer necessary to think in terms of a transcendental entity, to think of a goal of love outside of time and space. Love exists in the world and God is present at the moment in which you are actually feeling love. The whole theological emphasis beyond this world is reversed, inasmuch as the highest ideal is now to be found in a certain kind of attainment or self-realization *within* this world. That is related to the democratization in Romantic love. It is no longer to be thought of as reserved for philosophers or poets or saints. It is not delimited by traditional religion. It is a consummation, a completeness in terms of what people feel for each other as fellow participants in nature and because they are carrying out their individual search for goodness as human beings.

FULFORD: There's something really beautiful in that concept of love that comes down from the nineteenth century and the late eighteenth century. We've spent a long time, I guess, since the end of the nineteenth century, chipping away at it.

SINGER: Right.

FULFORD: And there's a kind of split that's developed between what you would call realism, on the one hand, and Romantic idealism on the other. Where does the realist critique of that beautiful ideal come from?

SINGER: Partly it comes from within Romantic love, and partly it comes from without. In the nineteenth century, ideas about Romantic love divided into two traditions—one of which I call benign romanticism, and that's what we've been talking about—and the other of which is Romantic pessimism. By the 1850s, many of the hopeful, positive, affirmative, Romantic ideas about the ability to experience love in this world were being questioned by various thinkers on purely Romantic grounds. Among the philosophers, Schopenhauer is the greatest example of a pessimist who says this is simply not the way the world is. There is something that can be called sexual or romantic love and it is extremely important in human life, but it is a trick on the part of nature to get us to reproduce. It should not be thought of as a quasi-religious phenomenon that happens between men and women. Instead, Schopenhauer argued, the amatory state manifests material processes that have very little to do with what people *think* is motivating them when they fall in love. As a result, a division along these lines developed within Romantic theory in the nineteenth century. But also there was a growing scientific awareness that possibly we need other categories of analysis in order to explain why it is that people become emotionally involved with each other. A great deal of what we recognize as behavioral science and the science of human relations develops out of this realist tradition that thinks of love in wholly un-Romantic ways. Freud is the foremost example of that in the twentieth century. But in a sense everybody who deals with what's called affective studies nowadays—that is, the study of how people respond to one another through their feelings—is more or less within the realist tradition.

FULFORD: I used to hear people say years ago, you're not in love with her or with him: you're in love with the idea of love. That was really an implied criticism, wasn't it, of what we've been talking about—the idealization of love.

SINGER: It's a criticism to the extent that if you tell a woman that you love her and it turns out that you're only interested in the idea of love, she has a right to be offended. She also has a right to be suspicious because if you're only in love with the idea of love then you could just as well make the same protestation to another woman tomorrow when you've got tired of her. There's always the danger that a relationship is going to be inauthentic or fragile if the man or the woman is more in love with love than with the particular person who has been designated as the recipient of one's love. I think that's true. On the other hand, however, you could defend the attitude by saying it shows that the nature of this concern is not merely sexual, and that it's not just the interest of a business arrangement such that you hope to get benefits from the other person for which you are prepared to reciprocate by giving him or her various compensations. If you are motivated by devotion to the ideal, your love can't be *totally* selfish or dishonest. But it's still very precarious.

FULFORD: But one thing it does is link you with this whole history of the idealization of love going back to courtly love and back to Plato. The idea that a person should be in love.

SINGER: Right. That's a very interesting and important point, because human beings are so constituted that they feel the need to identify themselves with great idealistic traditions. One of the reasons why people buy works of art, or reproductions, and put them on their walls is not necessarily to look at them. In fact, after a few days they probably become so habituated to these artworks they forget they are even there.

FULFORD: Yes.

SINGER: But they *are* there and they serve as a way of saying to oneself, and to one's friends, and sort of proclaiming to the world: I believe in art; I believe in this wonderful, creative ability that human beings have.

FULFORD: And I'm connected to the tradition this painting represents.

SINGER: Right. And that is supremely true about love. One reason we do love and feel a need to pursue love is because we believe that it promulgates an ideal that elevates human nature beyond anything it might otherwise be.

FULFORD: Thank you very much.

SINGER: Thank you.

5

Love in the Twentieth Century

Guest: Irving Singer
Interviewer: Robert Fulford

FULFORD: In terms of what has been written, thought, and said about sex and love in the twentieth century, surely Sigmund Freud is the embodiment of the most important set of ideas. How does a philosopher who deals with love approach Freud's work? I know you've dealt with him at least twice in your trilogy *The Nature of Love*.

SINGER: And differently. In the first volume I thought of Freud as defending an approach that is related to what I call appraisal as opposed to bestowal. By appraisal I mean the way in which people look for benefits in other persons that they can themselves enjoy selfishly; whereas by bestowal I mean people making one another valuable by means of the act of loving. I thought Freud misunderstood bestowal, failing to recognize it as a creative agency in life. Given his predominant interest in what people can get out of each other, Freud's insight was limited to appraisal. By the time I wrote the third volume I began to see the great wisdom and profundity in Freud, inasmuch as he realized better than his predecessors, I think, how important it is for people to be able to derive benefits from each other, how important it is for them to act in their own self-interest, how important it is for them to get goods out of each other that they cannot find anywhere else. I believe he is absolutely right about that. One can't hope for success in love or marriage or any intimate attachment unless the relationship is so constructed that each of the members will acquire important goods, benefits, values from each other. Bestowal is fundamental in love, and I am still convinced that Freud has no adequate idea of it. The ability to create value *by means of* the relationship itself is crucial for understanding the nature of love. But Freud was right as far as the importance of self-interest is concerned.

FULFORD: That, of course, set him sharply aside from the whole Christian tradition of love, didn't it, because in that tradition—which still exists, of course—the idea of self-sacrifice was very much a part of love.

SINGER: In Christianity there is a tendency to identify love with self-sacrifice. God so loved the world that he gave his own begotten son to save it. This sacrifice on the part of divinity, for no reason that we can fathom, is considered definitive of God's being. God is love and love is self-sacrificing. Freud has no respect and no tolerance for that attitude toward love.

FULFORD: When it's brought down to human life where one loves simply out of one's goodness, that would be presumably the human portrayal or acting out of God's goodness. For me to love someone must involve great sacrifice on my part.

SINGER: Whereas the Freudian tradition thinks of that goodness on which one's love is based as an expression of one's own self-fulfillment. It's good for oneself that one should love others, and that's why we're able to do it. It's not really self-sacrifice, but rather self-realization. This healthy-minded attitude is fundamental in all of Freud's thinking.

FULFORD: Freud, of course, is part—though the most important part—he's part of a much larger approach to love which is unique to our time. I mean scientism or the scientific approach to love, where one looks at love through psychology, even physiology, and so on. Has that changed the way philosophers deal with love?

SINGER: Very much so. I believe that is the great opportunity of the twenty-first century. If you start with the fundamental idea of health—healthy-mindedness, which I think is basic to psychoanalytic thinking—then the project for science and philosophy is to analyze what the nature of health is, what are the ways in which we can understand human development, individual development and social development that would maximize this healthy-minded capacity to love; and also what we can do in order to make the world more receptive to it. That's a very important task for philosophy, but also based on scientific investigations that give us facts about our social and material nature. This seems to me the hope of the future.

FULFORD: But there is a whole tradition of quantifying sexual expression which goes back to Kinsey and maybe beyond, where you add up the number of this or the number of that, and then twenty-five years later there's a Masters and Johnson tradition which—not limited to them in their clinic but spread over the Western world—which is a physiological approach to sex. Now isn't this narrowing down the whole business of man-woman or man-man or woman-woman relations?

SINGER: Well, it would be if one thought that by solving problems of sexology you're automatically solving problems about the nature of love. These are two different fields.

FULFORD: They're two different fields but one depends very heavily on the other.

SINGER: They can, and in fact I've been trying to do work in both fields. But I think of them as dealing with different kinds of questions. The sexological enterprise explains human nature in terms of sexual behavior and sexual instincts, to the extent that the instincts actually exist. The questions about love would be questions about how those feelings and how those sexual forms of behavior can be used. Once we understand what the nature of sex is, we can then answer questions about how it should be properly enacted for the sake of achieving relationships of love. The two enterprises can therefore be coordinated and suitably harmonized. But very little of this work has been done as yet. That's why I think of it as the promise of the future.

FULFORD: One element of this which comes up a great deal, both in public and I imagine in private, is the contrast or the conflict of lust versus love. Many, many people find that dealing with one without the other is very, very difficult. How does the philosopher approach such a knotty issue, a thorny issue, I should say, as that?

SINGER: Did you say knotty or naughty?

FULFORD: K-N-O-T-T-Y is what I said.

SINGER: It's both. I myself think that there's nothing in the reality of sex which in any way precludes the possibility of love. It's by means of our body that we're able to express our feelings and our attitudes. Sex is one of the most vivid and most important ways of showing love that we may have for another human being. It isn't automatic that by carrying out sex successfully we're going to achieve love, and it isn't necessary to use sex in order to express our love. Some people, for instance couples who've been married for many years, may have little of a sex life any longer but still enjoy a very rich love life. Some people can have very active and gratifying sex lives without a great deal of love. There is, however, the ideal of harmonizing the two which is the ideal of sexual love, and that is a magnificent ideal. In pursuing it, we function fully and completely as sexual creatures while also functioning fully and completely as loving human beings toward each other, toward the children who result from our sexual love, and possibly toward the world that sustains us in the ability to have this kind of relationship.

FULFORD: There is a very widespread belief—certainly expressed through the media and dramatic fiction—that loveless sex is much more present among us today than it was a few years ago and that somehow the love has been driven out of sexuality. Some of that may be the result of social conditions or whatever, but is it in any way a result of how we've thought about sex in recent years?

SINGER: Well, there's much more sexual experimentation, but there's little reason to think that the human race has flourished as long as it has without a great deal of sex. And much of that surely was loveless in the past. Whether there is more loveless sex now than there was before, I really doubt. Certainly there's more loveless sex among the unmarried than there was in earlier periods since relatively fewer people feel the need to get or remain married nowadays. On the other hand, I think those who have loveless sex are probably the first to say how much better it would be to have sex with somebody one does love. The ideal of sexual love—of a love that is sexual; of a wholly satisfying sex relationship that also involves love—is still quite strong today. It's just that people are freer to sample possible alternatives or methods of approach to the ideal, and often their experiments don't succeed.

FULFORD: The twentieth century produced many, many critiques of the ideals of romantic love that were left to us by the previous century. Perhaps one of the most striking came from all the existentialist writings of the last thirty to fifty years. The idea, really, in existentialism is that we're all so alone on this earth—perhaps I shouldn't be explaining to a philosopher what existentialism means. But it certainly presents a critique which adds up to the impossibility of love, because people are so alone and our isolation one from another is so great that it can't be bridged by this fiction of the nineteenth century called Romantic love. How have you tried to approach that?

SINGER: The best-known existentialist was Jean-Paul Sartre. But if you examine his life's work you find a very different kind of picture from the one you've described. What you've just referred to is true and accurate for his early period. Books like *Being and Nothingness* argue that, because of the isolation of individuals, love of a quasi-Romantic sort is impossible. In his later writing, however, he changed considerably. In a posthumous work that came out in 1983—*Notebooks for an Ethics*—Sartre develops an idea of love as an achievement of interdependence with other people. There he argues that human beings are such that their social nature impels them to seek, and sometimes attain, a kind of unity, a kind of oneness that can only occur as a result of love, particularly sexual love. In existentialism as a whole one finds these different strands. In the work of Simone de Beauvoir there exists a similar development. In her book *The Second Sex*—which has had much importance in feminist circles and for people generally—she emphasizes how women in male-dominated society don't have access to an authentic, genuine love; that's one of the evils of male chauvinism. But at the same time she holds out the hope that some day women will be able to experience an interdependence that will be authentic, that will recognize their autonomous differences from men, and that will be a complete, enduring, sexual love. So even in existentialism you get these different vectors.

FULFORD: You mentioned *The Second Sex*. In some ways it's seen as the beginning of feminist studies in the current period. But out of feminism—that book and the seven thousand that followed—there emerges a serious criticism of Romantic love and of the concepts of love by which our society lives. I know you've thought about the feminist critique. How do you deal with it?

SINGER: There again I don't see any single critique. I see a complex of problems that have elicited different kinds of responses on the part of feminists. Some radical thinkers—Ti-Grace Atkinson, for instance, in her book *Amazon Odyssey*—say that men and women are incapable of loving each other, that there's something in the difference between the sexes that makes it impossible for a man to love a woman or for a woman to love a man. But other feminists see this as the great challenge for our society; that if equalization existed and women were truly treated as the equal of men, then there might often occur a genuine love that would be very desirable. Still other feminists have claimed that men can't love, that there is something in the nature of male sexuality that orients it toward lust or toward appropriative sex even when it masquerades as love—that men just can't love: only women can. Still others hold that men and women can both love but women do it better than men.

FULFORD: That's a strong argument.

SINGER: Yes, it is. It seems to me that what Atkinson says is wrong—there does exist the possibility of authentic love between men and women—and that, in a sense, what the more moderate people say is also wrong. It isn't that love is impossible in our society but only that it is not as likely to succeed, is not as benign and as healthy a phenomenon as it would be in a condition of total equalization between men and women. So there again one finds a great hope for the future: that when women finally achieve equality, there may be a greater and better kind of love that men and women will share beyond anything they can have in a society that is troubled—as ours still is—by these questions about the relative status of the different sexes. As for the idea of women being better able to love, I think that's ultimately mistaken, too. Men and women are equal in this respect as in many others; they're both capable of love. Women experience love differently from men, partly because they are able to bear children and therefore innately possess certain nurturing capacities that men have to acquire through learning and experience. So there are differences between the kinds of love that men and women may have. But that's why it's important for them to join in mutual love between them: they can benefit from each other's kind of love.

FULFORD: One feminist critique, though, maintains that romantic love has cheated women. It really doesn't exist. It's a fiction. Women are sucked into it. As in a dream, they walk toward marriage and are then put in a subservient position, and it was love that did them in.

SINGER: I think there is some truth to that. Many women have identified with the aggressor—to use Freud's terminology—for reasons of love. They felt, well if I love the man then it doesn't matter that he sometimes treats me badly, that in general he doesn't act as if I were his equal, that I am forced to do things that he's not required to do, that I am expected to remain faithful but he can be free to range through other sexual possibilities; since I love, I should submit to it all. If that's the feminist critique, I believe it's correct. This isn't a criticism of heterosexual love, however—it's a criticism of the way in which it's been misused by women as well as men. In the case of the women, for reasons of their own weakness; strong and self-activating women are able to overcome this difficulty.

FULFORD: In recent times we often hear in relation to men and women the verb *merge*. Fusion is a part of the goal of many people who seek love today.

SINGER: Yes.

FULFORD: How do you react to that fashionable notion?

SINGER: I think the idea of merging is very unfortunate, even dangerous. Because it's an idea that in order to love another person, the two of you have to become some new . . .

FULFORD: Third.

SINGER: Yes, a third kind of entity in which each of you loses your individuality. I think this is foreign to human nature. I don't think one can lose one's identity. All one can do is to distort it in the attempt to merge. In order to explain love between human beings one needs a wholly different system of concepts. In the third volume of *The Nature of Love* and in my book *The Pursuit of Love*, I develop ideas about a sharing of selves, about interdependence as well as autonomy, about love as a relation that has nothing to do with fusion or merging between two people. I don't think the concept of merging explains the intimacy that men and women are really looking for. That consists in loving one another as separate individuals: they learn how to share each other's personality, they learn how to join forces in a common enterprise, they learn how to communicate effectively, they learn how to profit from an interdependence such that each can count on the other to be interested in one's own welfare. Above all, they learn to have faith in the sustenance and intimate corroboration that they can get from each other. This is a very exalted achievement. I'm not saying it happens easily, but when it does happen it provides all of the values that people think they want when they use the language of merging. The concept of merging is pernicious because it encourages men as well as women to submit and lose themselves, to forget what they really want or care about, and to evade responsibility for their actions.

FULFORD: In a sense the most exalted ideals about love in the nineteenth century were really the most popular ideals about love in the twentieth century, weren't they?

SINGER: Yes. There's a filtering down that always takes place in the history of ideas.

FULFORD: In the nineteenth century the poets and the novelists, perhaps (the serious ones), spoke of this exalted, beautiful ideal of love which today we find on the movie screen.

SINGER: Right. And I, too, think the ideal of sexual love is beautiful. It's a beautiful idea and it's a beautiful ideal, and it's one that ordinary people nowadays can feel they have access to in a way that they might not have at any other time in the Western world, and still don't have access to in many other cultures. Potentially, I think, it's an ideal that all human beings can honor and pursue, but in various societies it has not been tolerated or actively cultivated as it has been in the West. One of the advances of the twentieth century is the fact that this kind of interest was made available to so many people. But like every other good that becomes accessible, having been popularized, the ideal has been liable to misinterpretation and misuse. That's where philosophy comes in—to keep us on our toes. Progress means criticizing the past, particularly the way in which it has been appropriated by the present.

FULFORD: Yes. Just when humanity thinks it has things sorted out, there's someone such as yourself or the other philosophers in the long line who are there to tell us that that's not quite the way it is.

SINGER: The father of philosophy was Socrates and he described himself as a gadfly. And it's the function of the gadfly to keep biting, gnawing away at uninspected assumptions in the hope of getting closer to authentic truths.

FULFORD: But that ideal, that nineteenth-century Romantic ideal, is now the everyday content of Harlequin books, popular movies, soaps, and so on. What has replaced it at the sort of higher intellectual level where those poets of the nineteenth century lived when they were creating the Romantic love ideal? What's living there now?

SINGER: Well, I think we're still going through a period of digestion and critique, and surely some of the best poets are critics of the Romantic ideas. It is fashionable among our intellectuals to distance themselves from Harlequin romances and from soap operas. I don't read Harlequin romances myself and I don't watch soap operas. But I respect the humanity in them and I believe it presents a great challenge for philosophers: to make sense out of it. In that regard I don't despair of Romantic interests. I want to understand the workings of imagination and idealization in them, and I think philosophers should examine this, and every other way of pursuing love, with whatever analytical and scientific tools are now available.

FULFORD: Is it possible to say that we are still actually in the Romantic era? That when we put out books called *The Romantic Reader*, *The Romantic Period*, and so forth, we're still within that way of thinking? Aren't we?

SINGER: Yes, we're still preoccupied with questions that the Romantics raised. I think that's true. Incidentally, those questions are only about two hundred years old, which is not a very long time, given the number of generations that are involved, for thought to keep working at such problems. But we are tending, I believe, toward a new world in which those questions will be resolved.

FULFORD: Those questions, of course, dealt with many other things besides love. But what's the most important question that they raised regarding love?

SINGER: I suppose the most important question about love is whether human beings can have it in a nontheological setting, in other words without trying to orient their responses in ways that were previously dictated by the church or by religious traditions that claimed to have final, absolute explanations predicated upon extranatural truth. The question is whether human beings can manage on their own in a cosmos that may not be as friendly as previous generations thought. I interpret romanticism as part of the humanistic effort that encourages people to work out their answers for themselves, creatively and with freedom of self-expression. That, I think, is the greatest challenge of romanticism. But that, I also think, indicates the direction in which we're heading. Religious and spiritual ideas will have to be recast in terms of everyday truths that we discover on our own rather than dogmas that have been handed down by earlier authorities.

FULFORD: What is the future of love as an ideal? You know, you've chartered it as carefully as anyone ever has, through the minds of people who've lived over thousands of years; but you must've thought: Where does it now go from here?

SINGER: I believe it will involve the search for greater and greater personal enrichment, greater and greater recognition of the diversity of emotional values that human beings can enjoy. That's why pluralism is, for me, such an important approach in philosophy. In the pluralist attitude one doesn't assume there is a single correct answer to human problems. One doesn't assume that the human condition is unitary, or similar to problems in mathematics, for instance, for which you have to find the one and only right solution. In matters of our humanity there isn't any solution of that sort, and, therefore, there isn't any single answer to be found. There is only a series of explorations, and these vary from culture to culture, and from individual to individual. The function of the philosopher is to legitimize, and to clarify or explain, the ways in which a whole gamut of imaginative possibilities may all be equally plausible. This doesn't mean that every answer is acceptable, since you can have incoherent answers and you can have answers that are based on empirical falsehoods. Consequently there's room for the scientists to say: Oh, but this dogma has no foundation in what we know to be verifiably true; and there's room for the logicians to say: This or that notion is inherently inconsistent. There's room for criticism on the basis of these factual or logical criteria. But still one can tolerate a wide panorama of different responses, and that alone can have a great deal of immediate importance for social behavior. When I was young, there was a very limited range of relationships that human beings were allowed to enter into. If you didn't act in accordance with this limited range, you were considered either wicked or deficient or sick, and you were generally made to feel very uncomfortable. What I find as the present tendency, and what I foresee as the future for humankind, is a world in which an indefinite number of alternatives will be made available to men and women, the emphasis being on success within whatever lifestyle is chosen by each individual, as opposed to expectations uniformly imposed. In other words, even greater democratization, and possibly anarchy, in which persons and groups will be able to determine for themselves the way of life they want to have and pursue. Eventually the human race may manage to live up to this pluralistic ideal of love more than it has thus far. That's one reason I have written as I have—to encourage people (and myself) to find new, enriched, more creative, more imaginative ways of making sense out of our pervasive need to love.

FULFORD: Thank you very much.

SINGER: Thank you.

6

The Nature and Pursuit of Love Revisited

In 1991 a three-day symposium at Brock University in St. Catharine's, Ontario, Canada, centered about my philosophy of love. Twenty-five papers were delivered, mainly by professors of philosophy, theology, literature, psychiatry, and the life sciences. Most of these papers subsequently appeared in a volume entitled *The Nature and Pursuit of Love: The Philosophy of Irving Singer* (Amherst, N.Y.: Prometheus, 1995). My rejoinder, "A Reply to My Critics and Friendly Commentators," follows here somewhat revised. It gave me an opportunity to develop some new ideas about love and related matters which were elicited by the contributors to the conference. Quotations from the critics's and commentators's papers are cited by references to the relevant pages in the Prometheus volume. Though these essays are worthy of attention on their own, readers of the present book will find that my response to them is fully comprehensible in itself though, of course, selective.

❋

In view of the panoramic scrutiny accorded to my work at this conference, it may be appropriate to begin my reply with a somewhat autobiographical account of how that work developed as it did. On several occasions I have been asked how I first became interested in the concept of love. That is a legitimate question that one can put to any kind of philosopher. In my case it is especially pertinent since I have always striven very hard to make my writing an expression of my own experience *as* a writer, as well as someone human who exists in nature and in time. Apart from personal motivation that enters into all my intellectual efforts, I recall the importance in my life of a paper that I gave to the Philosophy Department at Cornell, where I was an instructor. It was on Plato's *Symposium*, which I treated as a dramatic vehicle rather than a quasi-scientific investigation. I interpreted Plato in that dialogue, and in most of his other work, as trying to organize ideas he found suggestive into an aesthetic whole, as opposed to making a consecutive analysis that solves problems and reaches some ultimate or definitive solution. I still think this is the most fruitful way to understand Plato's intention. At the time I gave the paper, I had discussions about its approach and subject matter with Gregory Vlastos, who was then a professor at Cornell. Like him I believed that Plato fails to appreciate the love of persons, and in fact that his philosophy of love seems to rule it out.

That line of thought eventually recurred in the first volume of *The Nature of Love* when its first edition appeared, and similar ideas were later developed by Vlastos in an article that has had seminal influence in the field. Whether he got these insights from me or I from him, I don't remember. I do know that when he read the first volume he wrote me an enthusiastic letter in which he remarked that the chapter on Plato was the best thing on the subject to have been published thus far. Though I was delighted that he should have said this, I also felt he was possibly being too generous, and I am willing to believe that my point of view was conceived under his tutelage.

My first article in the philosophy of love was the essay "Ortega on Love," which is reborn, much altered, in this volume. It contained some ideas that I have since discarded. But it also shows what I had learned from Ortega's emphasis upon love as a confirmation and sustenance of the beloved's being. Soon afterward I began reading Anders Nygren's *Agape and Eros*. That book provided my first acquaintance with the Judeo-Christian concept of *agapē*, which then nourished my initial speculations about love as bestowal.

For some time earlier I had been convinced that philosophers like Nietzsche, Santayana, and Dewey were right when they considered religious thinking of every sort to be imaginative and nonliteral speculation that is basically incapable of yielding factual truth. I took this as encouragement for my desire—which has been with me as long as I can remember—to discover the aesthetic truthfulness in religious or metaphysical writings as well as in great works of literature and art. It was, therefore, easy and natural for me to reinterpret the notion of agapē, to see it from my own humanistic perspective, to stand it on its head or rather (if I am right) on its feet in order to use it as a tool for understanding processes of imagination and idealization that belong to everyday life.

While this fermentation was growing in me, I remained what I had been trained to be, an analytic philosopher schooled in the methods and doubtless the prejudices of my Harvard education. I had studied with C. I. Lewis, Henry David Aiken, Donald C. Williams, and, to a lesser extent,

W. V. Quine, and like them I believed that only science can give us literal truth about the world, that rigorous analysis is essential for solving all conceptual problems that are capable of being solved, and in general that the unexamined life is hardly worth living. I have not changed much in these beliefs, but from Henry Aiken as well as friends and mentors in literature such as Walter Jackson Bate, I began to glean the possibility of dealing with problems of feeling and human affect as a whole in ways that were then being ignored by almost all reputable professionals writing in English.

I was also influenced by the later Wittgenstein, by ordinary language philosophy centered at Oxford, and by the final efflorescence of existentialist thought on the Continent. These were liberating forces, offering me an escape from the narrowness of American analytical philosophy even though I did not wish to renounce it completely. It spoke with rationality and clarity of thought in the midst of a world that seemed to clothe its confusion in verbiage that was mainly mystical and woolly-headed. Analytic philosophy stood firmly in allegiance with the newest developments in science and technology, to which it promised assistance not only in matters of their methodology but also in their moral and aesthetic implications. It aligned itself with thinkers like David Hume, John Stuart Mill, and Bertrand Russell—each of whom I much admired. From this aspect of my formation, and from the presuppositions of psychiatric authors as well as emotivists in ethical theory like Charles L. Stevenson and A. J. Ayer, who also belonged to this protoscientific mentality, my thinking about appraisal and bestowal evolved.

At first I was most intrigued by the idea of bestowal. It expressed my intimations about creativity, imagination, and the manner in which love and possibly all of life can be envisaged as an art form. I felt this opened up exciting prospects that suited my temperament as well as my particular talents, which were and are primarily aesthetic rather than deductive or casuistical. My orientation is apparent in the first chapter of the love trilogy's first volume, especially in the first edition of that volume. The concept of bestowal, which I introduce in that place, receives a formulation various readers have misconstrued. It was proffered not as a definition that gives necessary and sufficient conditions, but rather as a series of insights into love as related to modes of valuation.

Though I presented bestowal as a necessary condition for love, I did so in a philosophical equivalent of what an impressionist painter does when he portrays a field of poppies or a lady in a parasol as a manifestation of speckled luminosity pervading the visual world, or like Cézanne enabling us to savor the phenomenon of spatial depth by revealing it through the contrivance of a two-dimensional representation. I did not wish to suggest that love was *nothing but* bestowal. That kind of approach is alien to me. I see the world through very different spectacles.

A number of years before the first chapter was written, I had concluded that appraisal is both an essential ingredient in human love and a causal agent without which human beings could not love. At MIT in the early sixties, I gave a public lecture in which I explored my thinking about appraisal and bestowal. Some in the audience, particularly my colleague Hubert Dreyfus, complained that I was treating bestowal *almost* as if it were the sole determinant in the definition of love. I remember feeling grateful for my subsequent discussions with Dreyfus. They led me to see more clearly that each of the elements needs to be accentuated if one seeks an adequate and comprehensive statement about our capacity for love: both types of valuation have their varied role within it, and therefore love must be explained in terms of an interaction between them.

I was not yet able to depict that interaction in a way that would satisfy me, however, and in the first volume the role of appraisal does receive less attention than it deserves, and certainly less attention than bestowal. By the time I wrote the third volume, I realized how much more I could say about appraisal, and in *The Pursuit of Love* I try to clarify the relation between the two contributing elements by means of several different coordinates as required by a pluralistic analysis.

I am not saying that I have completed the task. I hope to continue working at it, digesting and possibly learning from new explorations that are constantly arising as life goes on. I have always felt that the doing of philosophy is a thing of the moment, like the eating of our daily bread. For me, at least, my earlier writings tend to seem dated, and occasionally stale, after a few years. I sometimes find it hard to think I had a hand in their creation. Yet I know I did, and I often feel that I could, and should, have done a better job.

An anecdote about a tenor performing in an opera in Parma may be apropos. Audiences in that Italian city are notoriously censorious about singers who appear on stage before them. On this occasion the tenor was both surprised and gratified when he received an ovation after singing an extremely difficult aria. The audience demanded an encore, and so he repeated the aria. Another ovation ensued, and another demand for an encore. This kept happening, until the tenor felt that his voice could take no more. Flushed with exhilaration and fatigue, he stepped forward and smiled as he addressed the highly receptive audience. "I am very flattered by your applause," he said, "but I have now sung eight encores of the same aria. How much longer must I go on?" To which a voice from the second balcony replied: "Until you get it right!"

I don't believe I will ever satisfy a standard as elevated as that. Nevertheless, I am grateful to the participants in the Brock symposium, and to those who did not participate but provided special additions to it, for reminding me of how much more work still needs to be done, in general by everyone struggling with our common subject, and specifically by me. The unfinished cycle of love-operas that I have been composing for so many years may never culminate with my getting anything right, but encouragement that the mere existence of these papers offers has helped me keep trying. The effects are already present in *The Pursuit of Love* and later books of mine.

In relation to bestowal and appraisal, I am fortunate in having benefited from criticisms that Russell Vannoy leveled against my distinction in his challenging book *Sex Without Love: A Philosophical Exploration*. I assigned that work as required reading in one of my courses and responded to its comments on my philosophy in the third volume of *The Nature of Love*. I had hoped that in the Brock symposium Vannoy would reply to my reply and thus allow us to keep the tennis match going. What he has done, however, may be of greater utility. In making the claim that love reduces to appraisal, rather than depending on bestowal or being a mixture of bestowal and appraisal, he touches on questions that properly force me to reconsider my overall theory.

As I interpret it, Vannoy's argument is the following: romantic, interpersonal love can best be understood in terms of appraisal, not only as a matter of causation but also as the sole and omnipresent determinant in the phenomenology of love itself. At his senior prom everyone sought out as possible objects of amorous relations not the undesirable boys or girls but the ones who were attractive, the ones who were amenable to each individual's personal self-interest and/or were valued highly by the group as a whole. At the same time, however, Vannoy recognizes that "passion that is aroused by someone's appealing qualities wants to escalate in intensity" (75). For this to happen, qualities that are only moderately beguiling come to be seen as more desirable than they really are. But "really" poses a problem in this context, and, therefore, Vannoy distinguishes between "reality in the phenomenology of the loveworld" and what we recognize as "ordinary reality." The latter is rational and purposive; the former indulges in those flights of feeling and imagination that would be illusions or even delusions in ordinary reality but that make a valid contribution to the reality of the loveworld.

If this were the total burden of Vannoy's analysis, there would be no major differences between our two formulations and I could wholeheartedly admire the inventiveness in his engaging mode of writing. But his distinction between the loveworld and ordinary reality is designed to show that appraisal *alone* explains the workings of each. That is what I find unconvincing.

Vannoy claims that while aesthetic imagination might bestow upon a baglady value needed for her to serve as a suitable subject for artistic appreciation, she is not likely to be the person anyone falls in love with. At the opposite extreme, it is the beautiful blonde cheerleader whom all the males at Vannoy's prom were in love with, or wanted to love, and, according to Vannoy, she felt the same about the handsome quarterback she finally married. Vannoy recognizes that there may be difficulties in loving a goddess like Marilyn Monroe, since she is too desirable and therefore makes one feel worthless. But then, as in the case of his mother's successive choice of seven husbands, Vannoy relies on the concept of what I call individual appraisal to argue that loving someone depends entirely on our finding in him or her just those qualities that may possibly satisfy our own needs and desires.

To me it seems clear that Vannoy's conception is overly reductive, like most attempts to discover a single principle of explanation for anything as complex as interpersonal love. Not only was the real Marilyn Monroe far from being a goddess, but also her image is alluring to many men because it projects a fragility and vulnerability that causes a certain kind of man (Norman Mailer, for instance) to bestow upon it, and therefore upon his idea of her, a value requisite for love to arise in him. This would be even more evident in relation to the blonde cheerleader at the prom. Her fetching qualities in the ordinary reality Vannoy describes might lead every robust boy to hunger for her love, or at least her sexuality, but crossing into the loveworld itself requires responses that are not wholly explicable in terms of appraisive considerations that belong to either reality.

The shy and pimply adolescent with whom the cheerleader deigns to dance will feel the stirrings of love, as distinct from mere desire, only when he perceives that she, too, is insecure in ways that he can appreciate, that for reasons of her own she needs his lowly adoration, that his acceptance of her as the person she is matters to her, and that this makes her more interesting to him than she could ever be as just a curvaceous fleshpot or symbol of the school's athletic standards. The new and greater interest that love induces results from the operation of amorous imagination, which may be present in all of us but is generally hidden or unformed until such time as there occurs a coalescence between individual development, social conditioning, and the good fortune of meeting someone who can help us to cultivate and express this innate potentiality.

For some people the essential coalescence may never materialize, just as some poetic geniuses may never write a word or sing a song that others can hear in societies that thwart such acts of the imagination. But the loveworld, which interpenetrates our ordinary reality even though it may be studied separately for the purposes of analysis, is of imagination all compact. Love, like the creation of meaningfulness in general, reveals the ability of life—above all, as it appears in human beings—to bestow value upon almost anything that catches our attention and makes itself available for this unique mode of self-realization. Without appraisal there would be no purposive behavior; without bestowal, life would not exist as it does in ordinary reality, for then there would be neither meaning nor love, and purposiveness itself would make no sense at all.

Seen from this perspective, interpersonal love directed toward a baglady becomes more plausible than it could ever be in Vannoy's philosophy. He chooses the baglady as an example of someone who is repellent, unattractive by usual appraisive criteria, and therefore unlovable. And, indeed, she is unlovable, if by that word one means difficult to love or lacking in the qualities that normally engender love in most human beings. But all persons, and all objects, are capable of being loved if one has a capacity for love great enough to accommodate them. One need only focus one's attention upon their individual qualities and accept these persons or objects as what they are.

Bestowing value in this fashion, we may find that we can delight in attributes that would ordinarily be distasteful. Every person can be loved despite his or her faults and imperfections. They become meaningful to us as the properties of someone who elicits our capacity to bestow. Human beings give great importance to this capacity, for it is deep in our nature and inherently very gratifying. We often treat the bestowing of value—by ourselves or by others—as an ideal condition that matters more to us than anything else in life. Why, then, should Vannoy doubt that some people can feel love for a baglady, or for many other individuals he disdains? Out of idealizations such as this arise mighty religions and moralities that civilization cultivates from generation to generation.

In Paul Gooch's paper on friends and lovers in ancient Greek philosophy, I detect a similar confusion about my notion of bestowal. In the course of making interesting statements about the limitations in Aristotle's idea of friendship, Gooch cites the importance of intimacy but then claims that it runs counter to the bestowing of value. "If I thought your love was added from nowhere," he says, "and if I seriously believed that my love for you was entirely a matter of my giving you a gift you didn't deserve, decent relationships [of intimate friendship] would be more fragile than they are" (89). Gooch argues that the intimacy he considers crucial in love can occur only if there is a "commitment to protect, cultivate, and nurture what's grown to be valuable in the other and in the relationship" (89).

Gooch is right in thinking that Aristotle tends to neglect this aspect of friendship and that he overemphasizes mutual admiration of the goodness that already exists in each friend. But Gooch ignores the fact that a commitment to "protect, cultivate, and nurture" what matters to the friends itself involves a bestowal of value that pertains to friendship love as it does to all other types. For there is nothing in what we judge a friend to be worth appraisively that requires us to commit ourselves to the furtherance of his or her values. That comes from nonappraisive motives in us and issues into an attachment or concern that no mere recognition of deserts can automatically elicit.

In that sense the bestowal of value that occurs in friendship is indeed an undeserved gift. This gift does not belong to the same logical order as gifts that are deserved—for instance, a box of chocolates given to a secretary who has worked after hours. The gift of love, the value that bestowal creates, is always gratuitous, determined inherently by no prior goodness that could require it to exist. There must have been causes for each bestowal to occur, and on analysis we may be able to specify how these involve appraisals related to needs, desires, and hoped-for satisfactions without which we could not survive in the world that we inhabit. The appraisive attitude must also participate in friendship as a constituent of the ongoing relationship, and whatever bestowal there is must always interact with this valuational component—either supplementing it, if it is positive, or else compensating for its negativity. But this only proves that bestowal and appraisal both have a role to play.

In friendship, as in all love, we delight in attributes that merit approbation. Yet in itself, by virtue of its own definition, such love is more than just the making or unmaking of positive appraisals. In expressing our delight, it bestows value in a way that is personal and largely unpremeditated, and therefore Gooch does well to emphasize the danger of its gifts being spontaneously "withdrawn." What that means, however, is that no friendship can be truly indestructible regardless of how meritorious the individuals under consideration remain. While bestowal is needed for there to be affective attachment without which love of any sort could not survive, no experience of delight or affirmative concern can guarantee its own perpetuity. Among human beings at least, bestowal depends upon psychological factors that are normally hard to control, and so its continued existence is always uncertain.

Perhaps my critics have had difficulty with the concept of bestowal (as I have as well) because it lends itself to so great a variety of explications. Appraisal seems relatively simple. We know that as purposive beings all people have desires and needs, impulses and inclinations in relation to either something or someone whose attributes may provide a relevant consummation. We therefore feel competent to evaluate this thing or person (or ideal), and sometimes even to set a price on it. Our evaluation is an "individual appraisal" if it is based on the other's utility for ourselves alone, as the ones who make the evaluation, or else it is an "objective appraisal" predicting what some community of evaluators would establish as the public worth of this thing, person, or ideal in relation to individual appraisals that might occur in a hypothetical class of equally purposive human or quasi-human beings.

Bestowal, as I have characterized it over the years, seems much more complex and elusive than either kind of appraisal. The truth is that in my pluralistic manner I have wanted to observe it as it varies in nature, to watch it as it flutters through reality rather than to snare it in a net like a butterfly one mounts as a relic next to other forms of life that have been killed and are now also on display. In my description bestowal involves benevolence toward its one or many recipients, for value is being created in them, but bestowal equally occurs as a means of enjoying and delighting in these objects of our attention, or at least some of their attributes. Through bestowal we accept them, not as we accept a trial offer of some household article that arrives in the mail but rather in treating them with respect and in recognizing a dignity in them they have not necessarily earned and that we accord them on our own. Their sheer presence in the universe is highlighted, given special importance. Our bestowal addresses itself to what they are "in themselves," as is and not in reference to whatever valuational ranking they may also merit from an appraisive point of view.

While imagination operates extensively in appraisal, it is more obvious in the creation of value that is central to the very nature of bestowal. Moreover bestowal adheres to the individual character of some reality, which appraisal may not do. Though everything is what it is and not another thing, appraisal cannot bother about such tautological verities. It is geared to the discovery and acquisition of goods needed to flourish as whatever organism one is. Many instances of the same type will function and satisfy equally well, and therefore there is little appraisive need to discriminate among them. That fact is built into our concept of a commodity. But bestowal sees *through* the commodityness of anything in order to attend to its uniqueness and autonomy regardless of how it can be used. Bestowal aligns itself with a disposition not only to *care about* but also to *take care of*. Although empathy, sympathy, and compassion are different modes of feeling and behavior, as I argue in *The Pursuit of Love* and *The Harmony of Nature and Spirit*, each of these attitudes reveals one or another of the relations between caring and bestowal.

Since bestowal issues into such a wide and intricate network of responses, it takes on different guises when it appears as falling in love; being in love; staying in love; interdependence; the love of things, persons, or ideals; the libidinal; the erotic; the romantic; the sensuous or the passionate; and so on through all the other aspects of our humanity that I try to clarify by using whatever distinctions come to hand, like tools in a workshop that have some usefulness at the moment. If I am pressed to organize these implements and their possible employment into a final unity—a single or total resolution of all ambiguities—I find myself embarrassed by a request of that sort. It seems artificial and pointless to me. My life and my experience have never allowed themselves to be regimented in so orderly and precise a manner. I might have been a more accomplished person if I had acquired at an early age the requisite habits. But for whatever reason, I did not, and the world as I have known it has always seemed to me somewhat random, highly vivid and creative in itself, but systematically defeating all attempts to package and squeeze it into the limited confines of a neatly unified scheme. Perhaps that is why I see reality as novel at every moment and always *re-creating* itself.

❄

In his attempt to explain what I mean by appraisal and bestowal, David Goicoechea says that with the passing years my ideas about appraisal have been "growing." That is equally true of my thinking about bestowal. My conception of both elements keeps changing, just as my lived experience does. In tracing the history of the idea of love, I likewise concentrate upon its own trajectory of change, from primitive naturalism to transcendental idealism to post-Romantic humanism, as Goicoechea notes. At the same time, I feel that the germs of my later thought are clearly present in the first volume of the trilogy. Even my insistence that bestowal must always be subjected to moral appraisal was already enunciated in my prudential remarks about the perils of unbridled bestowal and the greed of giving.

I do not, however, cite this combination of continuity and development as evidence of growth in the sense of *progress*. My work on successive instances of idealization may help me to understand an important region of mentality that humankind has evolved within a fairly short period of time, and they can tell me much about myself and the parameters of my own developing imagination. I, too, am a product of the human evolution manifested in the history of these ideas. But unlike Hegel, I do not believe that the Absolute has been marching forward with me or anyone else in mind as its chosen stopping point in the present. I agree with Nietzsche as well as Santayana in their revulsion toward the arrogance of such self-preferment.

My indebtedness to Santayana, despite my repeated criticism of his ideas about idealization, is discussed by Timothy J. Madigan, and Goicoechea elaborates upon my kinship to Nietzsche. At the time I wrote the chapter on Nietzsche in the third volume, I had little sympathy with his conception of amor fati. I still have great difficulty with any notion about our loving a universe that is mainly inanimate and apparently meaningless as a totality. I felt, and still do feel, puzzled by the suggestion that one might love the existence of gravity, the pervasiveness of thermodynamics, the elements in the periodic table, the forces operating in all molecular structure, or any comparable powers that are foundational in the universe. I can understand our having love for whatever there is in it that provides gratification to us. But this will not be a love of fated destiny or reality as such.

Nevertheless, what Goicoechea says about the affiliation between Nietzsche's philosophy and my own illuminates a facet of my thought that has become increasingly important for me since the third volume was written. Goicoechea points out that in my later description of appraisal's pervasive role in love I see that even the rejecting of the beloved implied by any negative appraisal can engender positive bestowals that may then interact with disapproval of this sort. And is this not, Goicoechea asks, similar to the cosmic love that the Nietzschean saint attains in loving the world although he believes it to be nasty, brutish, and hideous?

I sense the appeal of that suggestion, and in *The Creation of Value*, the first volume of *Meaning in Life*, I probe the conditions that might explain how someone could feel a "love of life," life in its entirety. In that book I also suggest that we can love the love in everything, which is to say, all animate existence as it strives to achieve a good either for itself or for something else. Although we can extend this love to reality as a whole only through a precarious extrapolation, I recognize that one might treat each individual thing or person or ideal as a *candidate* for love, as not excluded a priori from a love that we can feel even if the object of our love is incapable of experiencing love itself. This is less than Nietzschean amor fati, but it marks a step in that direction that I am comfortable in taking now.[1]

I think Goicoechea is mistaken, however, when he identifies Nietzsche's ideal with the love of God that Piccarda manifests in Dante's *Paradiso*. Her attitude presupposes the dichotomy between appearance and reality that Nietzsche sought to overcome throughout his writings. Piccarda confounds Dante by claiming to be close to the blessedness of God's being, since she accepts his will and finds her ultimate peace in that, even though she inhabits an outer circle of paradise and seems to be removed from the divine presence. It is precisely this distinction between appearance and reality that Nietzsche rejected, more brilliantly than any philosopher who preceded him, and that rejection elucidates both his notion of amor fati and the difficulties inherent in it. In my own development, Nietzsche's attack on religious ideas about appearance and reality had an enormous effect that shows itself in almost everything I have written as a philosopher.

❄

My radical repudiation of traditional distinctions between appearance and reality is the underlying cause of John McMurtry's complaints about my outlook. In the afterword to his paper, he responds to three of the criticisms I made to the earlier version that he delivered at the 1991 symposium. The first of them deals with the question of my "subjectivism." Without defining that word too laboriously, or even in the detail that I felt McMurtry should provide in order to strengthen his argument, I freely admit to being a subjectivist in the sense that I accept no system of good or bad that claims to have unique authority grounded on some nonempirical structure of Being and apart from the *making* of values that life itself is always enacting. Philosophers, such as Plato, who believe in objective standards generally do so because they think the world of appearance is too unstable, unreliable, and even illusory to yield a guide to what is truly valuable. In their estimation, only supremely rational insight into "ultimate reality" can do that.

These ideas have always seemed to me bankrupt from the start. They presuppose that the ordinary world is inevitably deficient in ways that force us to renounce it as a homeland to the spirit; they posit a nonverifiable realm of supernature that embodies a meaning of life that precedes rather than issues from the bondage we undergo in our cave-like existence on earth; and they deter us from understanding the infinitely rich and fertile activity of human imagination and idealization as they themselves generate values that burgeon throughout life that we, in our actual condition, consider meaningful.

In emphasizing the unity of appearance and reality, am I guilty of a dubious reliance on bestowals as McMurtry thinks? It is true I hold that, as living entities, we create whatever meaning there is in our own life. I believe that all human value—including the kind that love represents—originates to this degree from bestowal in one or another form. But McMurtry misconstrues the context in which my assertion occurs. He says that I envisage love as "essentially" bestowal of value; he states that my "introduction of 'appraisive value' in volume 3" is subjectivist in an additional sense, namely "in its confinement of value to what the loved one does for the lover alone"; and he concludes that I have no way of explaining how love can "extend further than the circle of lovers" (280).

But all this imputes to me a kind of subjectivism that is foreign to my thinking, and has been from its beginnings. I have never held that love is *essentially* any one thing. Even in the first volume, I described bestowal only as a necessary condition, and my distinction between objective appraisal and individual appraisal was intended as a means of establishing that love involves social and cultural interests as well as the needs or desires idiosyncratic to each of us as individuals. Appraisal that I call objective recognizes values that we inherit or acquire from the society in which we grow up. This kind of objectivity makes no claims to any ultimate or prior realm of values, and yet it reveals that much more is at stake than goods the lover gets from the loved one in isolation from all social or extrapersonal considerations.

I cannot deny, however, that the love trilogy—and, in some measure, *The Pursuit of Love*—neglects many of the questions about the cultural and biological implications of love that McMurtry finds most interesting. I hope that he and others will make up this shortcoming. My perspective and my vision are primarily literary and humanistic, in the sense of being concerned with the phenomenology of the good life rather than the resolution of issues related to social science or the logic of decision making. These questions warrant further attention and various approaches may certainly be defended, provided one gives up the search for transcendental, or otherwise metaphysical, objectivity.

This point is relevant to the last of the three criticisms that McMurtry makes. In effect he finds my pluralistic attitude unhelpful for the assessment of practical issues that love must always involve. I can see the sense in which he may be right. I have no authority as a counselor in matters of the heart. My personal failures and successes, sufferings and joys, have never seemed to me an adequate basis for telling others how to live. My own system of values is present in almost everything I have written in the last forty-five years, and those who know me well enough can possibly identify the individual reality that lies couched within my judgments and varied points of view. But though I treasure this source of whatever creativity I possess, I have no desire to use it to preach or to proselytize.

Instead I have wanted to make my ideas clear, hence the notion of "mapping" concepts of love which guides me throughout *The Pursuit of Love*. The task of reaching practical and justifiable solutions that all men and women need must be carried out by each of those persons separately. Apart from encouraging people to make their own ideas clear, and beyond any wise saws and modern instances that one can cite, I do not believe there are universal truths to which any philosopher has special access. As a pluralist, I am content to accept this limitation. It is a rule for playing the game cleanly and with elegance, a formal constraint that turns this mode of cognition into an art form.

In thinking about Marvin Kohl's criticism of my ideas about love in relation to autonomy, I begin to see implications of my pervasive pluralism that I had not noticed before. Kohl's original presentation, as well as his "postscript" to it, were extremely useful to me in the writing of *The Pursuit of Love*.

They led me to distinguish between freedom and autonomy in a chapter of that book, and to reexamine once again my belief that love involves an acceptance of the autonomous condition of the beloved. I am very grateful for the stimulus Kohl provided. My basic position remains unchanged, however, and therefore the differences between us have not diminished.

Kohl argues that a certain kind of love, which he calls "caring love," sometimes requires active intervention by the lover for the sake of assuring benefits to the beloved regardless of the fact that the beloved opposes such intervention. Kohl thinks that this kind of well-intentioned paternalism is indicative of caring love rather than a weakening of it, and he rightly suggests that on my view such behavior would have to be considered a lack of love. Certainly my concept of bestowal implies an acceptance of the other as is, as he or she is in him- or herself, his or her indefeasible autonomy being and remaining paramount in the loving relationship. But to say, as Kohl does, that I am thereby smuggling covert libertarian doctrine under the abstract pretense of a theory of love is unwarranted. Bestowal as I understand it implies no "commitment to . . . unencumbered private property . . . rights" (231). It only means that love ordains boundaries to the lover's benevolent attitude, and that his or her desire to benefit the beloved must be secondary to what this other person wants as a reasonably mature and autonomous being. Love, as I see it, inevitably excludes the kind of paternalism Kohl espouses, however moderate that may be.

What can be said decisively on either side? Are we just drawing lines in the sand as an expression of our differing world outlooks? It would seem that we are engaged in formulating what I call idealizations, each of us specifying ideals that matter to us individually and each articulating his own network of philosophic as well as personal bestowals. I am not opposed to that summation of our controversy, but I think there are appeals to disinterested reason that can also be made.

In *The Pursuit of Love* I depict the fragility of love and the fact that as an evolving condition in the lives of two people intimately dependent on each other it is always subject to destructive influences. One of these is the possibility that the other person does not understand or appreciate what one "really" wants. I put the loaded word in quotes because there may be no way in which participants in the relationship can be sure of what the other does want, or even of what they themselves want. They have sentiments, desires, inclinations with which they identify themselves, but all this occurs in a fluid and amorphous complex of vital forces that constitute every moment of life, particularly the life of human beings. The addictive smoker seems to want to kick the habit, but does she *really*? Neither she nor the husband who worries about her health and thinks his love requires him to be paternalistic can ever be sure.

Of course, there are many instances, a great majority perhaps, in which we have a pretty good idea of what the other wants, above all when she consistently tells us about her feelings. But there always lurks the possibility that she is deceiving herself or unaware of her true nature or even acting out a compulsive need created by the harmful addiction. To protect ourselves or others, or this person, we may have to intervene. But in the process we always run the risk of impairing the edifice of love. Just as the beloved may be deceiving herself in thinking that she wants what really she does not want, so too may the lover be deceiving himself in thinking that his paternalism is motivated by love rather than a moralistic attitude that will eventually undermine the loving relationship.

For love (at least the love of persons) to exist, and to last, each individual must benefit as just the person that he or she happens to be. It is in the name of benevolence that the paternalistic attitude arises in the first place. But if the lover's behavior is indeed paternalistic, it disregards by definition a value that for many people is the greatest benefit of all—namely, the goodness that consists in being allowed to forge our destiny exactly as we choose and with the assurance that the person we are most attached to respects the autonomy we cherish so much.

Is Kohl prepared to deny the validity of this interest? Is his moral stance so authoritarian and nonpluralistic that he is willing to claim that he or anyone else can ever legislate about the final goodness or badness of a person's freely chosen life, apart from its effect on others? Does he really want to maintain that self-determination is not an indefeasible value to which everyone has a right? Great crimes have been committed in the name of paternalistic love—think only of Cromwell's puritan tyranny or the Spanish Inquisition, both predicated upon a love of God, or the Soviet dictatorship that justified itself as a means of creating the love of humanity.

I do not know whether these remarks make my position more reasonable than Kohl's. It is possible that I am just adding new embroidery to my tapestry. But whether or not my argument sways a hypothetical third party trying to reach a decision, I have little interest in scoring polemical points. If I can articulate my vision with clarity and sufficient honesty, I will be happy to let the chips fall where they may. All the same, I realize that my view has consequences that many people will find unpalatable. If one believes that a desire to love requires us to accept anything the other person wants autonomously, this can include her desire to kill our love, to kill herself, or even to kill us. And isn't that an even greater contradiction, or paradox, than what I ascribed to Kohl's opinion?

I do not think so. Though love cannot be defined as self-sacrifice, it does involve a willingness to overcome any selfish desire we may have that the beloved serve only as an object of our own interests. If we want her to remain in love with us simply because we cannot bear the idea of living without her, ours is no longer an attitude of love. If we want her to stay alive regardless of her preferring death rather than a terminal medical condition, for instance, that causes her to live in terrible pain, we are not motivated by love. If we truly loved her, we would yield to the realization that she no longer wants to live.

Kohl's account addresses itself to the fact that love and benevolence are closely interrelated, the lover being concerned about the welfare of the beloved. And indeed, death is not a benefit. Death eliminates a life and cannot be considered beneficial to it. But *dying* may be, if that is what someone chooses under specifiable circumstances. The individual who thinks he is acting out of love although his behavior overrides what the other person is ready to accept, or condone, has deluded himself about the nature of love. Authentic benevolence, and therefore love, entails a willingness to forgo intervention deemed unwelcome by the object of our solicitude. If we impose our good will despite the other's expressed rejection of it, that may even constitute a paradigmatic example of loveless aggression.

I have greater difficulty dealing with the lover's acquiescence in the beloved's wish that he no longer love her or that he should even cease to exist. There may be a basic contradiction in situations such as those. They involve not only love as an acceptance of what the other is and wants, but also acceptance of her wanting to destroy one's love for her and possibly for oneself. Can nature endure such inner splitting of the vital roots? To love another person I must control my desire to help her if she does not want me to, but must I also harm myself and my sheer ability to love her if that is what she does want?

We may have reached a limiting case, the edge of the world of love beyond which one falls into nothingness. But in fact, I do not think the stated possibilities indicate a condition in which love must terminate. Though we may accept the other as she is and therefore sustain her autonomy, our love does not require us to negate our own autonomy. On the contrary, we could not love her or anyone else unless we remained faithful to what we are ourselves and what we want, which in this case means staying alive and loving her as best we can. If these conditions are unacceptable to the beloved, her love for us may have been destroyed, since she will not be accepting us as we are. But that is another matter.

In making his critique, Kohl raises a number of subsidiary issues that also need to be considered. First, he asks whether I hold one or another of two somewhat different ideas about bestowal: "the negative claim . . . that the bestowal of love does not seek to alter the object in ways that are alien or contrary to its own inclinations and desires" or "the stronger claim . . . that neither in the bestowing of, nor in being in, love is there warrant for intervention unless such an action is consented to" (231). Kohl says that he suspects my view is the latter. His surmise is correct but misleading. I make both of the claims that he refers to, but I do not mean what he implies.

Restating my position as he does, Kohl makes me sound as if I deny that the lover can want to change the beloved. In one place he says I believe that "loving another person we should *only* respect his desires to improve himself" (231). This is something I have never held. To do so would be to ignore the importance of the appraisive element in love. In accepting the beloved as he or she is, the lover affirms the autonomy of this other person. But that does not require forfeiting standards of good and bad, desirable and undesirable that the lover wants the beloved to live up to. These standards cannot be *imposed* upon the beloved, even if the lover thinks the beloved might benefit from having satisfied them. But it would be contrary to human nature for the lover not to want the beloved to have traits that are good rather than bad, desirable rather than undesirable. Playing on the ambiguity in phrases like "seek to alter" and "warrant for intervention," Kohl misrepresents the relationship between bestowal and appraisal as I envisage them.

Kohl thinks there may be sexist implications in what I maintain. He suggests that my "'autonomy talk'. . . seems to reflect a male story as opposed to a women's story of love" (232). I can't see why he says this. Mine *is* a male story, since I am a male, but it is not one that puts any woman's story of love in jeopardy. Of greater interest is Kohl's assertion that when it comes to "pluralistic welfare," as he calls it, dignity and autonomy are not always "trumps." But I never claimed they were. I was only giving a theory of love. I was saying that love, which does not comprise all of life or even all of the good life, requires an acceptance of the other's dignity as an autonomous being. Kohl himself recognizes that dignity and autonomy are necessary conditions for the good life and he rightly insists that intervention for the advantage of another person must never be allowed to undermine that person's sense of self-worth. But he fails to realize that acting paternalistically means subordinating respect for dignity and autonomy to the giving of goods that the other person may not value as highly as the benevolent agent does.

To the extent that we force our values upon others in this way, we are not acting out of love or engaging in an enlightened pursuit of it. Even if we think that they may end up having what they themselves will someday welcome as a better life, thanks to our paternalistic act, our behavior might never constitute a love for *them*. They may only be serving as a means to a well-intentioned goal we have in mind. This could reveal our love of some humanitarian ideal, but it would not be the same as loving another *as a person*.

※

In Stanley G. Clarke's paper I find an orientation with which I feel very much at home. Clarke characterizes love as a process, as I also wish to do, and like me he recognizes that it is "a process that is historical and not strictly natural" (237). Before considering how one should interpret these beliefs that we have in common, I want to revert to the question about the role of appraisal in love. In a paragraph that alludes to Alan Soble's examination of my philosophy in his book *The Structure of Love*, Clarke says: "Singer claims that appraisals are necessary conditions for love but not constituents or part of the definition" (237). As his reference, Clarke cites page 13 in the first volume of my love trilogy. If one studies that page, however, one finds a brief discussion that purports to show that love is "primarily bestowal and only secondarily appraisal," and that it "is never elicited by the object in the sense that desire or approbation is." I see my mistake in not explaining my use of the words *primarily* and *secondarily*, and in not having inserted *mere* before *desire* and *approbation*. I assumed, unwisely as it turns out, that these and similar statements of mine would be understood to mean that even the most favorable appraisals must be accompanied by affirmative bestowals in order for love to exist. Elsewhere in the same chapter I remark that human love includes both appraisals and bestowals, and that appraisals function as constituents within such love as well as being relevant to its causation.

Some of the conclusions that Clarke derives from his belief that love is a process seem to me quite doubtful. For one thing, he maintains that, "The search for necessary conditions tends to encourage one to identify love with only one part of the whole" (238). But this is like saying that writing on a computer makes one's literary style mechanical, or even that an interest in electronics will throttle one's aesthetic sensibility. We can find confirmatory examples in each case, but as generalizations neither of these assertions is at all plausible. The goals of the different values are not the same. They are easily separable and their competitive effect upon anyone's thinking or experience will vary greatly from person to person. Similarly, in questions of love, what matters most is how one uses one's definitional analysis to understand this affective process. When Clarke presents his own ideas, he himself occasionally seems to find the distinction between appraisal and bestowal helpful.

The crucial issue is what it means to think of love as a process. Clarke argues that science "cannot give us a complete theory of love, and that is because love is not only a process but a historical process" (244). This view is more extreme than mine was, since I held out the hope that eventually science might construct a unified and exhaustive theory of love. I failed to indicate exactly what that would consist of, and I am not suggesting that I can do so now. But Clarke's statements about the historicity of love, with which I agree, lead me to conclude not that science will never be able to offer an adequate conception but rather that it must move in directions that have hitherto been neglected.

Clarke thinks that since the historicity of love creates its "intractability for science" we must turn to literature or other humanistic fields for this element of a comprehensive theory. Though he may be right, it is interesting that he draws his example from the work of Turgenev, whose realistic approach to the art of fiction sought to emulate the descriptive methods found in science. Is there anything in Turgenev's account of first love or falling in love as a human phenomenon that cannot be studied scientifically? Turgenev would have denied that there is. He wanted to report about imagined human relations much as a naturalist in entomology does in writing about his observations of ants and termites.

In several places in my books I refer to a time when scientists and humanists will join forces and collaborate in an attempt to articulate a persuasive theory of love. Since Clarke seems willing to admit that psychology may one day give a scientific explanation of creativity, an aspect of reality that the humanities have always treated as their native province, I doubt that he means to exclude the possibility of such cooperation. But if it did exist, with scientists and humanists learning to appreciate each other's expertise and drawing upon each other's methodology whenever that is appropriate, why would the fact that love is a historical process pose a difficulty for this new science, or prevent it from attaining a complete formulation of its own?

Steps in this direction have already been made in routine investigations by psychiatric theorists, cultural anthropologists, personality psychologists, primatologists, ethologists, and others in behavioral biology. Sometimes in a crude and rudimentary fashion, which needs to be refined through better education at a preliminary level, these investigators already employ fragments of the humanistic imagination. The life sciences regularly deal with historical processes as revealed through case studies, autobiographical documents, anecdotal information, and even works of literature that are taken to include reliable data. As yet the scientific and humanistic communities have not sufficiently combined their resources in the area of love, or human affect in general. But one should not rule out the possibility that they may do so in the future.

My guarded optimism is developed further in *The Harmony of Nature and Spirit* and in *Feeling and Imagination: The Vibrant Flux of Our Existence*. In those books I speculate about the ways in which life is permeated not only by the creation of meaning but also by acts of imagination that are basic to our acquisition of knowledge about reality. I try to show that science depends on imagination (and idealization), just as art or literature does, in addition to whatever rational faculties are also needed. If this is true, our conception of how to attain a unified scientific theory about affective process must be altered considerably. The split between science and the humanities will have to be eliminated, at least in theory and consequently in practice more often than is now the case.

In John Mitterer's paper I find the beginnings of this desirable reconciliation between scientists and humanists. In several places, however, I feel that Mitterer overextends himself. Discussing male domination, for instance, Mitterer—unlike McMurtry—credits my work with having "laid bare the incredible depth of the problem" (249), but then he makes inferences that look to me like non sequiturs. In developing my suggestion that Plato's philosophy of love, like so many others, is an idealization that reveals fundamental values Plato believed in, Mitterer detects a psychology of domination as the groundwork of Platonic metaphysics. He may be right, and Plato's outlook is clearly interwoven with a male orientation the Greeks took for granted. But Mitterer describes the cognitive import of their view in a manner that seems rather simplistic.

Mitterer argues that male chauvinism in the modern world derives from Plato's antifeminine dogma, which he sees as an essential element not only in Plato's theory of forms but also in all subsequent metaphysical and theological thinking in the West. The traditional philosophy is thus shown to be a source of the psychology of inequality: "I believe that Singer's history reveals that the psychology of domination is undergirded by a metaphysic dating back to the Greeks" (255).

I myself do not find sufficient evidence for this statement. If Mitterer had said that earlier philosophies of love both presupposed and supported a sharp distinction between appearance and reality, or feeling and reason, or body and mind, that would have been more credible. But though the psychology of domination does belong to the world of everyday experience out of which traditional Western philosophy and religion emerge, it has no uniform role in their content. Even in Plato one finds aspects of egalitarian thinking, in *The Republic* as well as in *The Laws*, together with his more prejudicial assumptions about the sexes. In any event, one cannot derive male chauvinism from the theory of forms itself. The reifications built into that doctrine are such as to deny that men can be the ultimate objects of love any more than women. How, then, can the psychology of domination be undergirded by the resident metaphysics? If anything, the latter weakens the former, since human limitations in this area are thought to apply equally to both sexes. The same is true of Christian ideas about the primacy of God as both an object and a source of love.

All the same, the motive that leads Mitterer into these non sequiturs is one that I applaud. He calls for an alternative to the "grand schemes" we inherited in the twentieth century. He turns to the "mythopoetic" approach of Jung, Campbell, and Bly, among others, as possibly more relevant to our age than all the metaphysical systems of the past, however splendid they may still seem to some people. I recognize that as a wholesome attitude for someone who wishes to invent a world of ideas different from any that has yet occurred. And like Mitterer, I believe in the importance of fashioning what he calls "a naturalistic, humanistic psychology of equality."

But I am less sanguine about finding the needed sustenance in irrationalists like Jung or philosophically naive thinkers like Campbell, just to mention those two. The permanent merit and continuing utility in the work of great philosophers of the past, and of those in the present who identify themselves with them, consist in their strength of mind, their willingness to follow an argument as far as it will go, their talent for rigorous abstraction, and their love of truth as they understand it. In seeking to clarify concrete experience, and to appreciate insights that only empirical science can yield, we would be boxing with one hand tied behind us if we forgot the great achievements in the history of even metaphysical philosophy.

The writings of Sigmund Freud serve as a case in point for what I have just said. Pat Duffy Hutcheon's paper stresses, quite cogently, the influence that nineteenth-century philosophers, such as Hegel, Spencer, and Marx, exerted upon nonspeculative as well as speculative components in Freud's scientific work. In the chapter from *The Nature of Love: the Modern World* to which she directs her comments, I tried to systematize Freud's ideas about love and then to examine them critically as if they were the ideas of a philosopher. It is always perilous to deal with the thinking of a nonphilosopher in that way. One can never be sure that an alien discipline is not being imposed upon a creative imagination that is basically very different. I seem to court this danger more than most contemporary philosophers writing in English. I did so with Mozart and Beethoven in my book on their operas, with Kinsey and Masters and Johnson in *The Goals of Human Sexuality*, and with many literary figures in both of my trilogies and elsewhere. To the extent that this trope of mine is defensible, it would have to be defended anew in each place and with respect to the particular issues involved.

My suggestion that Freud be studied not only as a scientific theorist and investigator but also as a philosopher seems to me fairly innocuous. He clothed himself in that purple mantle on many occasions. The question is whether I deal adequately with his arguments and criticize him fairly. Throughout my work on love, he serves as a touchstone for the modern mentality into which I was born. Leaving aside my writings on Santayana and my unpublished undergraduate thesis on Dewey's theory of value, I have devoted many more pages to Freud than to any other theorist. In the first volume of the trilogy, I use him as the main example of what I called "the eros tradition" in its realist mode; throughout my writings on sex he represents a type of essentialism I pit against the essentialism of Masters and Johnson in my effort to reject both dogmas; and in *The Pursuit of Love* and *Feeling and Imagination* Freud is the focus of discussions about civilization, autonomy, and the need for nonmechanistic methods of understanding affect.

Possibly because she does not consider these other books, Hutcheon tends to misread me on several points. First she claims that Freud included in his theory something like my concept of bestowal. Since in the first volume of the love trilogy I recurrently cite statements by Freud that show he has no comparable view, this strikes me as very strange. Without repeating my detailed arguments, I can only say that Freud's notions of idealization and overvaluation of the object, which are central to his theories about love, derive from his belief that love must be a psychogenic distortion, an illusion and a cognitively unwarranted expenditure of surplus energy. Bestowal, as I understand it, is nothing of the sort—at least, not necessarily. It creates value in a manner that Freud does not acknowledge or fully recognize.

When Freud mentions "the act of loving" in the passage from *Civilization and Its Discontents* that Hutcheon quotes, he is referring to a circuitous tactic, as illustrated by St. Francis, by which we armor ourselves against the fear of not getting the love that everyone craves as a selfish constant in human nature. Freud is not modifying his usual claim that giving love must always be reducible to wanting to be loved. He is explaining how a particular way of loving can occur under special circumstances. Whether or not the concept of bestowal provides a better explanation, I see no reason to believe that Freud was employing an idea such as mine except (perhaps) at the peripheries of his more characteristic modes of thought.

Similarly, I think Hutcheon misunderstands the nature of my opposition to essentialism, whether in Freud or Plato or anyone else. I perceive essentialism not just as reification that obscures empirical realities, but also as an assumption that the world is well-organized in accordance with unitary categories that yield superior access to ultimate knowledge. It is not a question of determinism or biological programming that Hutcheon thinks I want to supersede by emphasizing freedom and environmental influences more than Freud did. My pluralism, or antiessentialism, is based on my belief that no system of analysis, no formula or mold of categorization, can fully indicate the diversity and equal legitimacy in radically different forms of both sexual response and interpersonal love among human beings. Ric Brown, who quotes from remarks about essentialism and pluralism in *The Goals*, seems to understand what I have in mind.

In part, Hutcheon does too. In one place she defends Freud's "attempt to seek commonalities or regularities in human nature." That is indeed what I was talking about in criticizing Freud. As against my approach, Hutcheon argues that "digestion and reproduction are similar the world over. Why not certain aspects of sexual development and associated psychic or behavioral complexes?" (190). But her implied assertion is either vague or a non sequitur: the former if "certain aspects" means that some are and some are not similar the world over, though we are not told which is which (or how much similarity is involved in being "similar"), and the latter if she is suggesting that it is reasonable to think that since digestion and reproduction manifest "commonalities and regularities in human nature," then the same must be true of love and sex. The complaint I make pervasively against Freud is not only that he fabricated grotesque icons of commonality and regularity, which Hutcheon believes as well, but also that he was mistaken in expecting to find commonality rather than diversity and regularity rather than idiosyncrasy as the basis of human sexuality and our incessant search for love.

Hutcheon wonders whether "social scientific inquiry" can proceed on attitudes like mine, so greatly different from Freud's in this fashion. I am unable to answer that question, but the mapping of the concept of love that I present in *The Pursuit of Love* offers itself as a theoretical framework for pluralism that social scientists might possibly find interesting. If they do, they may also want to inspect a further criticism of me that Hutcheon makes and that I find hard to refute. Defending Freud against my charge of dualism in his main presuppositions, she lists two things that she says I overlook: first, that Freud is monistic in the sense that he firmly believes all problems about human nature must be settled in terms of nature alone, without any transcendental or religious assumptions; and second, that all his distinctions are constructed with an almost Hegelian desire to show that opposing realities interact within a process that evolves dynamically in time.

In both of these comments Hutcheon is correct in what she says about Freud. When she maintains that I fail to recognize that "a passion for dichotomizing is not dualism," I feel the strength of her criticism of me. In stressing the effort of post-Freudians, and myself, to study human affect as a function of developing processes, I may have minimized the importance of this attempt in Freud as well.

That imperfection on my part, if it exists, is noteworthy in view of my own modes of thinking. Like Dewey, from whom I first learned how to express myself philosophically, I generally formulate my ideas in terms of dichotomies but then become suspicious of thinkers who turn them into rigid dualisms. As one who still resonates to the genius of Plato, I feel a need to "harmonize" the opposing concepts, to fit them into a broader and more highly integrated vision of reality. In discussing my search for harmonization, Madigan suggests that it sometimes turns my pluralism into a kind of trinitarianism. But the number 3 does not have a special fascination for me even though I find it inherently pleasing, as Hegel must have too, and therefore suitable for establishing a sense of reconciliation. For me, however, there is no final closure to the variant aspects of life, and that is what continually propels my thought into further expressions of pluralism. Given his doctrinal faith in scientific rectitude that should never be sullied by aesthetic excursions of this type, acceptable as they might have been in a separate compartment of his being, Freud must have seen his mission somewhat differently.

I am grateful to Ric Brown for two reasons. He realizes how important pluralism is in my thinking; and he is one of the few philosophers who still pay attention to my early book on sexological theory. Not that many of them did when the book first appeared. Compared to my other publications, it sold very well and was even distributed by two book clubs. But it was largely disregarded by my confreres in the profession, who seemed embarrassed by its mere existence. Others were also dismayed. Invitations to polite dinner parties in Cambridge, Massachusetts, and its environs immediately dwindled. On the other hand, my having written this book helped encourage Alan Soble to proceed with his efforts to create the Society for the Philosophy of Sex and Love, which became a part of the American Philosophical Association; and his including the initial version of my distinction between the sensuous and the passionate in the first edition of his anthology *The Philosophy of Sex* placed that much of my thinking about sexuality in the hands of working philosophers. Nevertheless, the main response to *The Goals of Human Sexuality* occurred among people in sexology and, to a lesser degree, in psychiatric theory.

In the early seventies the sexological world had been given a powerful jolt by the laboratory studies of Masters and Johnson. Radical feminists used them as a massive club to strike back at references to the so-called vaginal orgasm they charged Freud with having fabricated for his own sexist purposes. Investigators in the field began to sense the possibility of scientific, experimental work that had not been allowed previously. An exciting new approach to understanding human response in this area seemed to be opening up as never before. At the same time, there arose systematic doubts about Masters and Johnson's methodology, and various sexologists questioned some of their major findings. *The Goals* provided a theoretical, broadly philosophical framework of ideas that opponents of Masters and Johnson could use in order to make sense of their contrasting evidence. Whether it did so well or badly, the book served a function in sexology as well as in philosophy. It was philosophy in action, philosophy having practical implications for people doing scientific work.

For some readers it also had a more personal impact. One letter I received came from a woman whose sexual response had changed dramatically after she had a hysterectomy. She was deeply troubled by an apparent loss of excitation and by the fact that specialists she consulted assured her that Masters and Johnson had proved that sexual potential is unaffected by removal of the uterus. Her medical advisers intimated that her sexual problem was psychological rather than anatomical, which merely compounded her previous worries. After much distress, the woman encountered two doctors who suggested that she look at *The Goals*. They thought it might be relevant to her situation inasmuch as it argues, in its pluralistic vein, that uterine stimulation can have sexual and orgasmic importance to some women on some occasions. She wrote me that my book became a turning point in her life. It convinced her that she was depressed not because of extraneous psychological reasons but because she had lost an organ that was needed for a type of sexual response that she greatly enjoyed. Being a scientist herself, she later went on to write and publish technical articles about the sexological consequences of hysterectomies.

While *The Goals* had this kind of gratifying reception, entering the lives of at least a few people, it was nevertheless an exploration into a realm that skirts my principal interests. I did not and do not have the aptitude needed for continuous scientific work, and I assume that some of the physiological and biological details on which *The Goals* relied have now been shown to be mistaken. How much of the underlying theory would have to change in order to accommodate later empirical research I do not know. I am glad, therefore, that Brown's paper concentrates on philosophical problems that transcend the specifically sexological issues. He shrewdly zeros in on two related difficulties that are troublesome in my general outlook.

One of these deals with my distinction between the sensuous and the passionate. This has had a little history of its own that I should mention. The distinction was originally formulated as a conceptual tool for doing the sexological work *The Goals* undertakes. But I also suggested—and in *Mozart and Beethoven: The Concept of Love in Their Operas* I tried to demonstrate—that differences between the sensuous and the passionate can have significant philosophico-aesthetic ramifications. In the latter book I studied them in relation to operatic expressiveness. My venture serves as a backdrop for Marc Widner's paper, which illustrates Mozart's ability, in his piano music as well as in his operas, to express feelings that I characterize as either sensuous or passionate.

This way of approaching works of art is fraught with methodological problems, and possibly the major difficulties Brown adduces in his discussion of *The Goals* may also be applicable to *Mozart and Beethoven*. Brown's most telling point touches on my attempt to be even-handed in distinguishing between the sensuous and the passionate. If I am indeed a pluralist, as I continually insist, I should treat the two elements as, in principle, equal candidates for acceptance by different people on different occasions as they differently prefer. And yet, Brown remarks, my writing seems to reveal that I have "a clear preference for the passionate mode" (302). Nor does he mean that I, as the particular person I happen to be, prefer the passionate, but rather that my philosophical utterances presuppose its basic preferability. Brown then goes on, in a very judicious way, to show how I answer this charge both in *The Goals* and in the last volume of the love trilogy. But still there lingers the possibility that since I say that "something in valuation itself . . . engenders the passionate," I must consider it to be closer than the sensuous to the nature of love. If so, am I not tilting the scales to that extent?

I would be if I were a Romantic extolling passion above all other human interests. That, however, is not my view. Not only do I perceive that there can be equally authentic, albeit calmer, bestowals that constitute sensuous love, but also I am wholly aware that although there must be something in valuation that creates passionate response, this response can be a massive distortion of love and harmful to the individuals involved as well as to others. The sensuous always runs the risk of being overly cool and, therefore, lacking in the interpersonal sensitivity that love involves. But the passionate, in its fevered yearning and mindless ardor, can also render love impossible. As a philosopher, I wish to map out the alternate implications of the sensuous and the passionate. A priori, at least, I see no justification in favoring one over the other. On the contrary, it is because I treat them as equal components in sex or love, or the good life as a whole, that I study their ongoing interaction and speculate about conceivable harmonizations between them.

This brings us to the second difficulty in my thinking that Brown explores. It comes down to wondering whether my search for harmonization is really compatible with the pluralism I defend in *The Goals* and, as Brown points out, develop further in the various distinctions I sketch in the last chapter of the love trilogy. If Brown had considered *The Pursuit of Love*, particularly the chapter on sexual love, he could have mentioned more examples of both my pluralism and my probing into the conditions for harmonization. But do they ultimately conflict with each another? Whether or not my work succeeds in harnessing these different vectors, I do not see any necessary incompatibility between them.

As a species we are all divided into disparate motives and inclinations that are always clamoring for attention as if nothing else could really matter in life. The essentialist muffles the cacophonous din by choosing one of the voices in the human spirit, anointing it as authoritative, or even god-given, and then sacrificing everything else to the supremacy of this value he or she has thereby created. I rebel against such bigotry and raise my pluralist banner as a testament of my desire to love the love in everything. At the same time I recognize the authenticity in our typically human need, which is aesthetic and moral as well as purely cognitive, to quiet the perturbation of the vying forces by harmonizing whatever is indeed compatible within them. The impulse to experience the peace and unified beauty that comes from harmony is also something the pluralist can respect. In his paper John R. A. Mayer shows that he understands the role and the importance that this search for harmonization has had throughout my writing.

The outcome of a disposition such as mine must always seem wishy-washy and occasionally vague, as Brown contends. It may also lead to much suffering since the world can easily manipulate to its own advantage the ecumenical goodwill of the guileless and all-embracing pluralist. I have no easy solution and no foolproof recommendation, except that one should remember that some things worth knowing about oneself and others can be learned only by suffering. Let us not fear it unduly.

Reading over Brown's paper, I found it suggestive in relation to a question that he does not ask but that is very pertinent: Is my philosophy basically realist or idealist? I use that distinction throughout the historical parts of the love trilogy, but which of these alternatives applies to my own thinking? I can answer only in a halting manner. Insofar as I seek the harmonization of interests and admire it when it occurs, I must place myself with the idealists. I feel the grandeur of their quest and am sure that life without it would have less value. But though my writing struggles with questions about the making of ideals and their significance in human nature, I know that the sensibility I have just described is only my own. It reflects something deep in me that others may not experience as I do. In fact I think that most of life operates on a level that idealists have usually misunderstood, and that realists are often right to condemn them as self-deluding, even pompously overblown. Can the idealist and the realist perspectives be truly harmonized? I try to accomplish that in my work, but I would be reluctant to say that I am anywhere near this promised land.

Since the future is the past reconstituted by the present, I have always sought to integrate the philosophy I thought I was writing for coming generations with my explorations in the history of ideas. Here again was a dichotomy that had to be harmonized, and from the very beginnings I strongly believed that a good life for civilized men and women would include the love of earlier achievements in literature and the arts, together with a steadfast desire to build an aesthetic culture that creatively renews itself. Like Santayana, who was for me the model in this approach, I wanted to do history as only a working philosopher can and philosophy as only a historian of world outlooks would. Being someone who enjoyed the play of imagination, I relished its magnificence in my forerunners. What could not be acceptable in its literal intention might nevertheless be stimulating and inspirational as metaphoric insight or even artistic truthfulness. I was convinced that abstract forms of speculation can be as beautiful as, I am told, mathematics is. One had only to *humanize* these different disciplines, to see them as expressions of life on earth in its relentless and often pitiful craving to find meaning in a universe that may otherwise be meaningless.

To scholars who care about the detailed investigation of texts and their origins, this predilection may well appear amateurish. I think that some, perhaps a considerable portion, of it is. I often began my historical work in a spirit of general education for myself, which I then hoped to awaken in others by showing how much it meant to me. I never attempted an exhaustive presentation of some author's total output. I only looked for nuggets of idealization that would explicate and also redeem whatever philosophic point of view I had discerned in them, however flawed it might be in its development or unacceptable in its conclusions.

For that reason I originally heard, and then read, with keen appreciation the papers in the Brock volume that deal with my interpretations of historical figures. In several cases I felt that the commentators misconstrued, to some extent at least, the perspective from which I approached a particular writer. For instance, in his defense of St. Thomas Aquinas, Walter Principe both understands and does not understand my difficulties with the concept of merging. He rightly states that I find no way of making literal sense of religious talk about "mutual indwelling" between God and the human soul, though I acknowledge the poetic and nonliteral significance of what is being said. But Principe explains my difficulty by suggesting that I have "imposed a material metaphor of physical containment on the highest spiritual intercourse"(136).

I deny that I have done so. I meant to show how chaotic and possibly confused is the language used by St. Thomas and, of course, by Principe himself, when they refer to this "spiritual intercourse." They say it is a "sharing in the divine nature" but they do not indicate how this is possible without a loss of human separateness. It is as if a log consumed by fire can still somehow remain a log. Principe claims that the persons of divinity do not coerce the human agent in giving it the ability to love, since they just "wisely and lovingly guide" it, thereby allowing it to retain "real, if relative, autonomy" (137). He insists that there is no coercion—the Holy Spirit only "modifies" our being.

One might as well suggest that a chemical that causes permanent brain damage and consequent hallucinations has merely modified but not coerced the person who imbibes it, having only guided him or her into another mode of being while leaving intact his or her real though relative autonomy. In the case of the chemical we would be tempted to sneer at such a misuse of language. In the case of divinity allowing a creature to share in its loving nature, we do not sneer because the sentiment is so uplifting and we feel that the inexplicable metaphors reveal a wonderment in life. That is what lures imagination into this particular type of poetry. We must only recognize it for what it is.

Principe holds that between "metaphorical language and 'literally' being in one another" there is "the proper (and not metaphorical) ontological or metaphysical reality of union through knowledge and love without destruction of personality" (140). The nature of that "reality" is what he thinks I do not comprehend. But my problem is more extreme. I fail to find any justification for this use of language beyond the fact that it provides aesthetic values that may possibly help some people go on living.

These values are in principle the same as those that are made available to us by great music—not only music like Bach's B-minor Mass or Mozart's Requiem but also music like Beethoven's last quartets or Mahler's Ninth Symphony. In theological discourse, as in these musical instances, creative inspiration organizes bits of ordinary experience into a crafted whole that shows us how to enjoy the mystery of being alive as vibrant creatures in a cosmos that fills us with awe *because* we cannot fathom its enormity and its scattered splendor. I am willing to leave the matter there and to relish whatever beauty or insight I can garner from this typically human situation. Those who wish to arrogate for themselves the further dignity of being respectable both as philosophers and as religious adherents must demonstrate that their utterances make sense in everyday language.

In taking this stand, I have no desire to denigrate attempts to analyze love from a religious point of view. After a public lecture on "Nature and Spirit" that I gave at the University of Madrid in January 1994, the professor of metaphysics there remarked with quiet amusement that I sounded like a philosopher of religion. The idea amused me, too, though I did not tell him why. In my first academic appointment, at Cornell, I had been hired to teach philosophy of religion but then scandalized some members of the department as it existed at the time by announcing that I had no religious faith myself. When the first volume of *The Nature of Love* appeared, I thought that its humanistic approach to religion would elicit the hostility of those who did have religious faith but that it would be greeted by fellow philosophers. I was wrong on both accounts. The philosophers ignored the book and it seemed to survive in those early days only because people who took religion seriously found some merit in it.

I put into the first volume ideas in religious philosophy that had long been forming in me. For many years afterward, I felt that there was nothing more for me to say in this area of inquiry. Only recently, in working on *The Pursuit of Love*, did I encounter new thoughts welling up as a continuation of what I had formerly written. It was therefore very gratifying to discover that Graeme Nicholson thought my chapter on *nomos* in the trilogy worthy of his attention as a biblical scholar.

In his paper Nicholson goes far beyond my own remarks about the Bible, but in the issue about the union between man and God, where Principe and I have trouble with each other's thinking, Nicholson expresses my intention with clarity and exactitude: "To love and to know God," he says, "is to be desirous of the ever-continuing way into ever-increasing intimacy and concourse" (106). This implies no notion of melting or merging between the human and the divine, and it suggests a sharing of selves that seems to me indigenous to interpersonal love of any kind.

Nevertheless, I wish to quibble with Nicholson's reference to our "knowing" God. Since I, at least, can hardly understand what is signified by the word *God*, I cannot imagine what it would be like to *know* him (or her). Surely it is not like knowing the person who lives across the street. God's personhood cannot be knowable in any usual fashion, and in its ultimate being presumably not at all. But if the nature of that personhood lies beyond our comprehension, as many authorities would say, I wonder what one gains conceptually by thinking that God is even a person. In order to remain faithful to much of what religious people care about, I can *give* a symbolic meaning to the word *God*—as, for instance, whatever there is in the universe that creates and sustains us at every moment. This does not encompass all that devout believers wish to affirm; but the amorphous residue of theological discourse, which has meant so much to so many others, is not pertinent to my own experience and has no immediate reality for me.

❅

In John Nota's paper I detect some of the sources of my alienation from the religious mainstream. Presenting Max Scheler's philosophy of love sympathetically as he does, and rectifying my having treated it only briefly in the trilogy, Nota points out that according to Scheler "love, as the act of the person, is itself spiritual" (197). He contrasts this with my idea that we can love inanimate things as ends in themselves, and that loving another person means recognizing the degree to which that person is also a thing. This difference between us can probably not be surmounted. To me it seems like sheer presumption (to use the Christian concept) for any philosopher to define love as wholly spiritualistic. Love exists in nature just as vegetation or locomotion does. It emanates from the realm of matter as an organic process that pervades much of life, possibly all of it, and in human beings it is interwoven with imagination and idealization that constitute our search for consummation and for meaning. Love may contribute to, even define, the life of spirit, but in none of its variations can the love that human beings experience be adequately explained in terms of spiritual realities apart from nature.

For this reason, I find philosophers like Scheler and Nota powerless in their desire to understand love that exists in daily life. They are like Antaeus, the giant whom Hercules defeats by holding him aloft and thus separated from his mother earth, except that in their puristic thinking Scheler and Nota effect this separation themselves. To me that seems wholly unnecessary, and very unfortunate. It leads to a subtle form of impiety toward one's material source. Nota cannot see why I extol a love of things, or love that is "expressly sensual or sexual." In this approach he finds a contradiction in terms. He insists that love is always a love of persons, and he says that persons ultimately exceed or transcend their physicality. The second of these propositions is true, but the first is not. And neither does the notion of transcendence entail a condition that excludes the physical. Persons are not reducible to things, but nevertheless they are *also* things.

In one place Nota gives an erroneous account of my ideas which may have been a slip of the typist but is actually quite revealing in itself. He says that I, like Kant, think "one should never use a person as a means to an end" (201). Inadvertently, no doubt, Nota has omitted the word *merely* before the concluding phrase. It is indeed central to my conception of the love of persons that another not be used merely as a means to an end. If one does do that, one's relationship is something different from a love of persons. But among real human beings, as opposed to hypothetical deities, it is impossible to love persons as nothing but spiritual entities. Lover and beloved are both products of the material condition to which they belong. To undergo love as it occurs in nature, which is to say the only kind that we ourselves can actually experience, we must accept one another as inhabitants of the natural order and even as commodities, though not as *mere* commodities. We have no other means of attaining a love of persons.

Holding this view, which I develop further in the *Meaning in Life* trilogy, I analyze and defend the love of things in ways that elude the Christian philosophy of Nota or of Scheler. Nota says that things must be treated as subordinate to persons, just as nature is subordinate to God. He believes that our love of God enables us to love other persons as well as everything that inhabits the subhuman world. But since we can know and enjoy only this world and those other persons, can love be anything more than an acceptance of them as they are in themselves, as just the things or persons they happen to be?

Nota does not deny that "sensual or sexual" love may be compatible with a love of persons. But he thinks that happens only when the former becomes "an accompanying aspect of spiritual love." This misrepresents the fact that men and women are by their nature sexual as well as sensory, and so we can love them as persons only by accepting and appropriately responding to those elements of their being. Moreover, at its best, sexual love itself becomes a form of spiritual love. There is nothing in either to prevent their coalescence.

Spiritual love can also involve interests that are not especially sexual, as in the love of humanity or of life wherever it occurs. Spirit may possibly try to love all things that exist, as many mystics have wanted to. But even at its highest reach and moment of greatest success in this endeavor, spirit still remains a part of nature. Spirit may rise above the world but can never leave it. Nor would spirit attain its ultimate goal by doing so. Spirituality cannot be love unless it bestows value upon persons, things, or ideals as they are in nature. If we accept them only insofar as they have a subordinate role within a preordained system of spirituality, we falsify their inherent constitution and make it impossible for us to love them spiritually, or any other way.

In saying this, I do not doubt that our love for material objects must sometimes be subordinated to a love of persons, and that both may have to be subordinated to a love of ideals or divinity. But a priori at least, these different recipients of love are equal as candidates for bestowal and idealization. Each of us must decide for him- or herself about priorities to be established among them. The justification that can be given for choosing one or another hierarchy of importance will vary under different circumstances. It is not knowable in advance.

I can understand why a theologian may be appalled at a statement of this sort. Since God is the ultimate Being in all existence, how can any other object of love be given priority? But the premise of such reasoning must always have its origin in a personal faith that this reasoner already has. It is not a faith that I myself have ever had.

While arguing for pluralism at this level, it is clear to me that my view is antagonistic to the doctrine of a theorist like Kierkegaard. Sylvia Walsh's paper makes that point with exquisite awareness. She begins by remarking about the superficiality of my treatment of Kierkegaard, to whom I devote just a few pages, although he wrote so many on love and although I give a great deal more space to Nietzsche, who did not write much about it. Walsh is herself a true scholar, compared to a quasi-dilettante like me, and her informed feeling for Kierkegaard's mentality shows what can be learned from someone who is more sympathetic to his views about love than I am.

Apart from this confession of my limitations, I can only remind my critics that I was writing philosophical history, a study of past achievements in the history of ideas which emanates from interests relevant to my own philosophy in the present. That is why Nietzsche receives so much more attention than Kierkegaard. Even when his ideas flounder, as they often do, Nietzsche speaks to my soul in a way that

Kierkegaard does not. In giving her superior formulation of Kierkegaard's thinking about religious love, Walsh reveals but does not appreciate why this would have to be the case.

There are two fundamental notions in Kierkegaard that totally separate his thinking from anything I can consider defensible. The first involves his belief that Christian love is not only the highest form of love but also that it is *qualitatively* different from "purely human forms or expressions of love" (168). Walsh relates this claim to Kierkegaard's assertion that Christian love is eternal instead of being transient, and determined by action rather than feeling or passion. But these alleged properties seem to me subsidiary to his saying that only Christian love is genuine love, since only it can overcome the selfishness in self-love. All adherence to natural or "pagan" love is condemned on the grounds that it cannot eliminate our selfishness. Only Christian love is valid, according to Kierkegaard, because it alone is predicated upon self-renunciation, which he considers a necessary condition for love to occur.

This conception of love does not mesh with my sense of reality. Like Luther, I doubt that human beings can truly renounce themselves. Their attempts at self-renunciation usually result in self-deception, self-mutilation, and frequently the deceiving and mutilating of others. There is an insidious narcissism, to which religious devotees are often prone, in giving so much importance to our selfishness that we deem it worth destroying entirely. Only people dazzled by the bright but blinding light of their own idealism would construct such an ideology. Only they, as in the case of Kierkegaard, would be capable of the self-hatred that must fuel a desire to annihilate this basic component of their natural state.

To me it seems obvious that human beings, like all other animals, are self-oriented in the sense that they cannot survive unless they think and feel and act in pursuit of their own purposive interests. That is why, as Walsh remarks, the concept of appraisal plays so great a role in my philosophy of love. If we were gods, or capable of merging with divinity, appraisal would lose all importance except as a stage on the way to perfection. Since we are finite, mortal creatures, however, even at our most spiritual, we cannot hope to break the mold in which we have been cast by nature. The most we can do is to redirect or reshape it in accordance with ideals that transform nature while acquiescing in it.

Love is an attempt supremely of this sort. In bestowing value upon its object, it causes us to acknowledge the fact that others are also self-oriented and that what matters to them really does matter. In accepting them as they are, in respecting their autonomy and treating it as indefeasible, we compensate for our native selfishness. We cannot, and may not want to, eliminate it completely, for a love that does not benefit the lover as well as the beloved is not likely to endure. It may even be sick or immoral. And though love controls selfishness, and sometimes succeeds in curtailing it, love does not undermine or weaken self-love. On the contrary, it strengthens it. As Plato taught us, self-love is not the same as selfishness.

Kierkegaard also recognizes the difference between selfishness and self-love. But he interprets self-love not as self-affirmation or acceptance of one's being in nature, which is all that I mean, but rather as personal devotion to a God who is love. This leads to the second major difference between us. Unlike me, Walsh believes Kierkegaard is immune to my opinion that Christian idealization of love for God precludes there being an authentic love of persons as they exist in the ordinary world. She insists that Kierkegaard thinks of God as the third person whose presence makes it possible for the other two in a love relation to surmount their innate selfishness and thus to accept each other as just the persons that they are.

At the same time, as Walsh also notes, Kierkegaard states that God is the ultimate object of all love and that other persons are to be loved not as separate individuals but rather as part of a class comprising the humanity God loves. Kierkegaard even holds that loving oneself *means* loving God and, in Walsh's words, "the true conception of what it means to love another person is to help that person to love God" (172). These being Kierkegaard's beliefs, I do not see how his ideas about the love of persons can even be coherent. Though he says that God is the intermediary that initiates all other interpersonal love, his notion is inconsistent or chaotic insofar as he maintains that only God can be the *true and essential* object of love. Kierkegaard explicitly asserts that human beings can be loved not as the persons they happen to be but solely because God loves them.

Walsh concludes that for Kierkegaard love of God and love of persons are "integrally connected; one cannot have the one without the other" (177). But she fails to recognize that Kierkegaard's desire to transform the temporal into the eternal annihilates the preconditions for any human love of persons. Kierkegaard claims that loving another as one's friend or spouse means loving him or her primarily as one's neighbor or fellow member of the human race, and, therefore, that all distinctions between individuals are secondary and inessential for love. On my view, Kierkegaard's theocentric religiosity must be taken as a case of throwing out the baby with the bath water, as my teacher Henry Aiken would have put it.

In wanting to direct humanity toward a spiritual love that makes life worth living, Kierkegaard diminishes, not enriches, the quality of life as it occurs in actual men and women. That consists in our self-fulfillment as just the particular persons that all of us are, units in the class of general humanity no doubt but also separate from one another and each striving to solve interpersonal problems as they arise throughout our life together. These temporal necessities can eventuate in spiritual achievements that are real and significant, as when love of any type flourishes in a moral order that supports it, but this means only that "the eternal" is itself a consummation of our being-in-time. If we treat the temporal and natural condition of actual existence as merely secondary or inessential, we destroy the possibility of experiencing not only a love of persons but every other love as well.

It was because Ovid and Friedrich von Schlegel, each in his own period, emphasized the significance of the temporal that I included them among the humanist philosophers. In his paper on Ovid, Kevin McCabe argues that "the attitudes expressed throughout the Ovidian corpus are essentially the same" (116). That was the position I also adopted in the first edition of the first volume of my love trilogy. But when Winthrop Wetherbee, at the University of Chicago, saw the manuscript for the second edition, he called my attention to the many places in which Ovid speaks in a voice that differs from the one I heard. I began to feel that there was more to Ovid than I had realized, and I revised the text extensively. Instead of criticizing his writing as I had done, having assumed it was all an elaboration of sensuous interests that exclude passionate and marital varieties of love, I found a greater diversity in his different statements. My former reading of Ovid now seemed to me prissy in its condescension toward his love of the sensuous, and unjust in its delineation of his overall vision.

McCabe's paper does not commit the first of these faults, but I think he neglects the authenticity of Ovid's admiration for wholesome married love in the *Metamorphoses* and the *Heroides*. As a result, McCabe deprives himself of a fringe benefit that I culled from the change in my interpretation. Once I recognized that Ovid was capable of portraying and commending at least a fictional version of love between husband and wife, I felt that I better understood his influence on courtly love in the Middle Ages. Not only did medieval courtly love seek to idealize Ovidian relish for the purely sexual or wholly sensuous but sometimes it also professed ideals of married love. In his variegated pronouncements, Ovid could then be seen as a precursor and sustainer of these alternate directions within courtly love.

In Schlegel I discovered related windows of opportunity. I avoided the mistake of reducing his novel *Lucinde* to the level of tasteless pornography, as so many of his contemporaries—and even Schlegel himself in later years— seem to have done. The book was useful for my purposes because it focuses on the temporal as Ovid had, but then imbues the temporal with spiritual capabilities beyond anything Ovid would have imagined. And above all, it seeks to interpret human love as a search for health or healthy-mindedness.

This saving grace, this creative contribution in *Lucinde*, is greatly understated in Robert L. Perkins's fascinating paper. At one point Perkins does quote Julius, the novel's protagonist, as saying that only health is worthy of being loved. But then Perkins does nothing with this except to remark that "no Nazi eugenicist would disagree" (153). Since I, like Schlegel, was and still am trying to discover an adequate conception of love as a means by which human beings can attain a healthy immersion in nature, I underscored those aspects of Schlegel's novel that adumbrate this modern approach within the context of the nineteenth-century movement I called "benign romanticism."

At the same time I was aware that there are also components of "Romantic pessimism" in *Lucinde*. Perkins studies them in relation to criticisms by Schleiermacher, Hegel, and Kierkegaard. But the last two were hostile critics whose judgments are not always reputable, and Schleiermacher perceived the affirmative as well as the negative aspects of Schlegel's book. Unlike Kierkegaard, Schleiermacher welcomed its attempt to overcome the split between pagan and spiritualistic types of love; unlike Hegel, he could tolerate many of the utopian implications of Schlegel's ideas about an ideal relationship between man and woman.

Perkins discusses the places in which Schleiermacher disagreed with Schlegel, and they warrant his scrutiny. But for me *Lucinde* is important in the history of ideas because it points the way to efforts, such as mine, to define spirit in terms of nature, to explain successful love as a fulfillment of organic needs rather than as a supplanting or renouncing of them, to use concepts of health to show how love can be a beneficial condition that human beings may possibly experience here on earth and in our present dispensation. The differences between this kind of romanticism and the branch I call pessimistic are dramatic, even strident. Pessimistic romanticism despairs of the likelihood of happiness through love, denies that love can ever resolve the conflict between individuals, between the sexes, between lovers and the society to which they belong. Instead of associating love with a quest for health, Romantic pessimism generally sees it as disease and a pursuit of death, as in the Wagnerian concept of *Liebestod*.

Given the great divergence between these two types of romanticism, *Lucinde* must be classified as an exemplar of the former even though it contains elements of the latter. Nor should there be any ambiguity about my analyses of both or adherence to either. Perkins does me an injustice when he says that my description of benign romanticism "suggests that [it] may be [only] . . . self-indulgence or self-improvement, at best, or a manipulation of the beloved for one's own benefit, at worst" (150). There is no reason to believe that benign Romantics like the early Schlegel thought that love was confined to these two parameters. And neither do I. Perkins complains that my notion of appraisal sounds too "crass" as an insight into love. But life itself is crass, and anyhow bestowal—which Perkins does not mention—is there to make up the deficiencies of appraisal.

In general I do not identify myself with either kind of romanticism. Nor is my philosophy particularly Romantic. Although I analyze love as both the pursuit and creation of meaning, I do not think it is necessarily an eternal or holy substratum of life. Unlike the Romantics, I feel no inclination to reverse the Christian dictum that God is love. And unlike most Romantics, both benign and pessimistic, I do not assume that love is always socially or even morally justifiable. I know about the cruelty, deceit, and outright evil that may eventuate from love and that many lovers believe their powerful needs or passions authorize. I see no reason to commend such behavior, to dignify it in idealistic language, or to deny its underlying heartlessness and lack of decent sentiment. I have no desire to excuse the hurtful potentiality of love by pretending that it inherently shows forth spirit working its way through nature and transforming it into divinity.

All love, including the love of persons, is capable of causing a great deal of misery—not only in those who undergo the experience but also in those who are rejected or abandoned as a result. Artists who glorify love in song and legend have understood this as well as moralists who systematically condemn it. Those who are Romantic normally think that love justifies whatever sacrifice is exacted from oneself or others. Whether a Romantic is optimistic or pessimistic about love's survivability in the world as we know it, he or she is certain that it is worth any price one must pay for it (and make others pay in different ways). This faith, like all religious belief, is nonverifiable and often pathological. It is not a religion that I share or wish to encourage indiscriminately.

❈

The Puritans and the Rationalists of the seventeenth century, whom John Mayer discusses in his paper, interest me because they too recoiled from romantic love when it is immoral or excessively self-indulgent. This did not prevent the Puritans, at least, from enjoying the pleasures of sexual passion whenever these could be controlled and enclosed within the bounds of marriage. On the contrary, the Puritans (like the Victorians) learned how to turn restraint exacted by demands for privacy and social decorum into a means of intensifying their passionate sexuality. Wearing a corset can make one breathless. At the same time the Puritans, the Rationalists, and many of the Victorians correctly perceived that this consummation of their sexuality may sometimes become a flame that destroys everything else worth cherishing in life.

Having learned this from the Puritans and the Rationalists, I respect the horrified realism that pervades the philosophies of love in Schopenhauer, Freud, Proust, and the early Sartre. I have long considered Proust to be the greatest of all philosophical novelists, in view of his unparalleled ability to detect problems of philosophy embedded in the concrete actualities that he depicts throughout his fiction. But Proust has also been a puzzlement to me. While I admire his analytical and creative powers, I distrust the system of values—many of them unexamined—from which they arise and which they continually express. I have a similar problem with Wittgenstein. As much as I relish Proust's brilliant insights, I come away feeling that his project fails because he ultimately remains a *philosophe manqué*. He shows us how close a literary genius can come to being a philosopher, but he is not fully equipped to do the work of philosophy. This is not true of Wittgenstein, of course. In his case I sense a throttling of his literary susceptibilities which undermines much of what he would have liked to achieve.

Sartre would seem to have had a sufficient supply of both talents. His philosophical and literary capacities were ample, and each was developed enough to avoid the limitations in Proust and in Wittgenstein. But despite his ambitious efforts, Sartre stopped writing before he could finish his culminating work in either philosophy or literature. He never completed the major undertakings of his maturity, and he withheld his *Cahiers pour une morale* (*Notebooks for an Ethics*) because he knew it needed considerable revision and rewriting, though he felt he should not prohibit its publication after his death. As a consequence, Sartre's philosophy of love is extensively articulated only in *Being and Nothingness*, which he finally renounced when he recognized the basic inadequacy of its approach to human relations.

In my chapter on Sartre in the third volume of *The Nature of Love*, I tried to show the failure of his early philosophy as well as the positive promise of his inchoate later speculations. At the time I was writing I was one of the few philosophers to have seen that Sartre's ideas about love belong to three different stages, and that the last one contradicts the approach in *Being and Nothingness* for which he is famous. The paper that Thomas Flynn delivered at the Brock Symposium acknowledged the nature of my contribution.

In its written version, Flynn's paper makes some criticisms that should be answered. At one point he rejects my claim that Sartre's treatment of love has no proper understanding of bestowal. Flynn refers to the fact that Sartre talks about the "supreme value" a lover finds in the beloved. But this value, whether or not supreme, must be appraisive, since Sartre presents it as inherent in the lover's wanting to be loved by someone who treats him as an absolute. The passage in which my remark occurs is part of my discussion of *Being and Nothingness*. When I reach the ideas in the *Cahiers*, I point out that Sartre's philosophy of love had undergone a sea change by then and that attitudes of acceptance and rejoicing in the particularity of the Other, which do indicate an idea of bestowal, are accentuated as never before. Nevertheless Sartre's latter-day suggestions, which I welcome as corroborations of my views, remain casual and far from adequately analyzed by him.

Flynn also ignores the extent to which my work fleshes out many of the other skeletal and loosely written intimations in the *Cahiers*. One of them that I find intriguing but unacceptable is the notion that love consists in a tension between wanting to attain a merged unity with the beloved and wanting to preserve one's independence. I reject this approach, in Sartre as in the books of Robert C. Solomon, because it implies a belief in interpersonal merging which makes their conception seem inept. In *The Pursuit of Love* I develop my critique of merging further than I had at the time that Flynn was writing. In that book, I detail tensions in the phenomenology of love which Sartre might have recognized as similar to the ones he possibly had in mind but did not examine thoroughly. I study the ambivalent feelings many people have nowadays, simultaneously searching for love as a source of meaning while also avoiding it. This difficulty in the human predicament Sartre understood as well, I think, as anyone ever has.

Some of the other comments that Flynn makes about Sartre's philosophy in relation to mine are very helpful. He remarks that for Sartre love is linked with the doing and giving of one's work (*mon oeuvre*) and that "the paradigm of this generous act is artistic creation" (215). That is something I should have discussed in my chapter. It shows what Sartre learned from Proust, and possibly it explains why his ideas about interpersonal love go astray much as Proust's do. But also it elucidates the role that socioeconomic theory plays in Sartre's general philosophy, including his philosophy of love. Flynn says that if he has "one broad criticism" of my writing it is my "tendency to overlook this socioeconomic dimension of love as 'lived'"(218).

I think this criticism is fair. It shows the limits of my talents and imagination. Had I been more *engagé*, like Sartre, or preferably like Dewey, I might have been a better philosopher and perhaps a better philosophical critic and historian. On the other hand, if either Dewey or Sartre had been more accomplished as philosophers of love, I might possibly have avoided the pitfalls and the potholes that have slowed me down. For all his attention to values and the nature of valuation, Dewey does almost nothing with the concept of love, and his occasional mention of sexual motivation is very primitive. Sartre's involvement with socioeconomic realities as well as those that derive from his devotion to his art did not enable him to solve any of the problems about love that he confronted throughout his intellectual life. I know that one can profit from Sartre's experience as a philosopher. But as Hutcheon quotes Santayana as having said about the existentialists: "Is all this really necessary?"

That brings us back to my beginnings. In his paper Timothy J. Madigan discusses the continuities between Santayana's philosophy and mine. Still I have always been a critic of Santayana's Neoplatonism and its effect upon his aesthetics as well as his philosophy of love. As Santayana complained that Dewey was a half-hearted naturalist, so too do I feel that Santayana was a half-hearted materialist. Right as he was in seeing that spirit can exist only as an emanation of psyche, which is itself a principality within the realm of matter, Santayana is divided in his appreciation of the love of things. As a novelist and literary critic, and as an observer of human experience (including his own), Santayana has a highly advanced awareness of how the love of things operates in life. Yet as a philosopher of love, he subordinates it to the love of ideals in a way that falsifies our ability to love things, persons, or even ideals. Despite his superlative understanding of the fact that imagination permeates our entire being, Santayana's Neoplatonism persistently prevents him from seeing how creative our imagination can be when it helps us to bestow value upon things and persons as well as ideals.

What I learned most of all from Santayana was the profound importance of the humanities as an interdisciplinary resource in all intellectual pursuits. His writings taught me that in the life of the mind there is no absolute chasm between philosophy and literature, the two academic fields that have meant the most to me. In the Brock volume no one says much about my philosophical literary criticism. By way of conclusion, I feel that I should mention it briefly. At times in the past my work on the myths and legends of love has greatly preoccupied me. Someday I hope to return to it, to revise both published and unpublished chapters on that subject, and finally to finish the book for which they were originally intended. If I can, it will be in emulation of what Santayana was able to achieve, at a much higher level, as a humanistic philosopher writing in the tragic and largely loveless twentieth century.

7

Sympathetic Intuition: Henri Bergson

Bergson's thinking has not greatly affected English and American philosophy. Despite the early efforts of William James, few of our major philosophers have really taken him seriously. Even the devastating attacks by Russell and Santayana were polemical more than anything else, bestowing upon Bergson little of the precision and technical care these philosophers reserved for each other. Important as it was on the Continent, the Bergsonian influence survives with difficulty in our culture, just as the art of mime has rarely flourished in Anglo-Saxon countries.[1]

I mention mime because I think one could go very far toward understanding the special character of Bergson's philosophy by studying the practice of a great artist like Marcel Marceau. Bergson and Marceau have in common more than just an interest in movement. The crucial thing is the way in which they refuse to break it into discrete components, or to deal with it abstractly, as in physics or classical ballet. Furthermore, they have a similar approach to the nature of affect. Each of them investigates methods for conveying feelings as "directly" as possible—that is, without the interference of language and with a certain use of the body that treats it as a vehicle of preanalytic communication. I will not pursue the analogy further, but perhaps it can serve to remind you of obvious differences between the tradition to which Bergson belonged and the technical philosophy in which we have been schooled in the United States and Great Britain.

I myself come neither to praise Bergson nor to bury him. What particularly interests me in his philosophy is the concept of intuition. This, however, is so pervasive throughout his thinking that to do it justice would require an examination of the entire Bergsonian system. That being impossible, I limit myself to two representative problems that Bergson resolves with the help of his ideas about intuition. The first deals specifically with the nature of movement, the second with sympathy and the love of humanity. These problems are related as overlapping questions in metaphysics and moral philosophy. By working at them, as they connect with each other, we should be able to reach some insight into Bergson's conception of what I am calling sympathetic intuition.

Bergson distinguishes between two ways of considering movement, both of which are present in ordinary experience. One way is to think of a moving arrow, for instance, as traversing successive locations in space. Since the arrow is first here, then there, then somewhere else, there will also be a series of moments in time during which the arrow's movement takes place. This way of thinking about motion Bergson assigns to what he calls "the intellect." That faculty divides the world into discontinuous units that are useful for purposes of survival but actually falsify the nature of things. Treating motion in terms of points in space and time is thus allowing the intellect to break up reality into a set of immobilities.

Between any two of these immobilities, intellect will always be able to distinguish another and another and another. As a progression from point to point, movement would have to consist of an indefinite number of tiny jumps from place to place, each jump requiring an infinitesimal amount of time. This, however, overlooks the fact of continuity in movement. We do not see the moving arrow leap from point to point, and far from perceiving units in a trajectory we see the movement of anything as a single indivisible event. Intellect's way of analyzing motion must therefore be illusory.

The alternative that Bergson offers is what he calls "intuition." It occurs in everyone's awareness, he tells us, but is all too often smothered by the intellect. Philosophy liberates our intuition, much as Socratic dialectic was designed to help people to recognize what they really believe. In the case of movement, intuition fixes upon "pure mobility"—which is simply continuity itself, movement as we experience it apart from all consideration of units in space and time.

Bergson believes that while pure mobility also exists in time, it has a time of its own: "duration" or lived time. Duration cannot be divided into moments or any other elements of analysis. Divisible time is just an artifice of the intellect, its divisibility depending upon the divisibility of space. When we say that five minutes have passed, or five seconds, we are always saying something about units in space—for instance, the angles described by the hands of a clock. When we focus upon duration, however, we find nothing but a seamless flow, unitary, undivided, thoroughly continuous. Duration is itself pure mobility. We apprehend the true nature of movement to the extent that we live in duration. Since intuition is the sensing of duration, it alone reveals the moving, changing reality of actual experience.

Now it seems to me that much of what Bergson says is quite convincing. He argues that a statement like "my hand is moving from the table to the book" cannot be translated without remainder into a conglomeration of statements about points in space and time. He wishes to refute the position that Russell takes in his attack on Bergson. Motion, Russell says, "expresses the fact that a thing may be in different places at different times, and that the places may still be different, however near together the times may be."[2] By means of some such formulation, Russell insists, one can—as he says—"perfectly represent" a continuous motion.

Who is right? Bergson or Russell? As far as Russell's translation is concerned, it seems to me that he overlooks precisely that reality which Bergson is so keenly conscious of—namely, the phenomenon of continuity itself. When I speak of my hand moving from the table to the book, I mean something more than the fact that my hand will be at different places at different times and that the places will still be different regardless of how close the times may be. I also mean that between the beginning of the motion and the end, that is, from the departure at the table until the arrival at the book, my hand will not *stop* moving. If it did stop, in midpassage for instance, we would say there were two movements instead of one. Within each movement, however, there would still be the absence of any stopping point; there would still be the fact that my hand was *continuously* progressing from terminus to terminus. In a statement about motion there is something that cannot be reduced to an analysis of the sort that Russell gives. It is not enough to talk only about points in space and time.

The deficiency in Russell's analysis becomes especially clear when we think of what happens in the perception of motion. When I see my hand move from the table to the book, I see that it was originally in one place and that it is eventually in another and that this progression has taken time. But also I see something that I can only refer to as the continuity of a progression. If I stopped along the way, the progression would be discontinuous, broken up at the stopping point. But I would still perceive continuity within the resulting movements.

Imagine that you closed your eyes while my hand was at the table and then opened them again after it had reached the book. You might then say, quite rightly, "I notice that your hand has moved." You would never say that you had actually noticed the movement itself. You would have observed that the hand was in different places at different times, even though you had kept your eyes shut only a few moments. What you would not have observed is the fact that, from the time it started to the time it stopped, my hand was continuously moving from table to book. As far as your perceptions are concerned, the hand could have popped out of existence while it was at the table and then popped in again at the book shortly thereafter. In effect, Russell's analysis leaves open this magical possibility. To that extent it resembles the occasionalism of someone like Malebranche. The strength of Bergson's position consists in his supremely empirical refusal to relinquish an obvious component in phenomenological experience—the sheer continuity without which we could not see movement in the way that we ordinarily do.

In arguing against any reliance upon "what is called *experienced* continuity," Russell claims that "there can never be any empirical evidence to demonstrate that the sensible world is continuous, and not a collection of a very large finite number of elements of which each differs from its neighbour in a finite though very small degree."[3] He cites the stroboscopic effect to illustrate how movements that we perceive may really consist of many successive positions the eye is unable to recognize as such. What he does not appreciate, however, is the simple plausibility of hewing to the datum of continuity as something that is immediately apprehended under conditions that are inherently *different* from those of cinematography, and hence that ordinary perception does not lend itself to the reduction he proposes.

But though Bergson does well to insist that continuity is continuity and not another thing, his ideas about mobility lead him to further conclusions that are less attractive. For in continuity he thinks he has discovered "real movement" that exists in duration as opposed to the illusory movement intellect constructs and locates in space. And this seems to me as unacceptable as anything Russell may have said. Continuity is not the same as movement. It *belongs* to movement just as a straight line belongs to a square. Continuity is a necessary condition for there to be movement. But it is not a sufficient condition. Nor is it the only necessary condition.

In talking about motion, part of what we refer to is the fact that no matter what units of space and time you may choose, the moving object will never be limited to any unit of space or time smaller than its total trajectory and shorter than its total temporality. In other words, the following conditions must be fulfilled: first, that for every unit of time there is some correlative unit of space in the sense that if the object were stopped at that time it would be located within that space; and second, that regardless of how many space-time correlations you may determine, there are always an indefinite number of other correlations that would be equally good for describing what is happening to the moving object.

Though these conditions may seem to resemble those in Russell's analysis, they are significantly different. They are phrased as contrafactual conditions in order to stress the fact that the object never is stopped. Moreover, these are not sufficient conditions—which Russell's formulation requires. While he uses ambiguous terms like "expresses" and "perfectly represent," Russell wants to provide a translation strong enough to reject the Bergsonian emphasis upon sheer continuity. I am suggesting that Russell's attempt is out of touch with reality.

For his part, Bergson would never treat any reference to space and time as a necessary condition in our awareness of continuity. He would argue that mobility exists as a distinct and indivisible phenomenon. He would claim that the units I mentioned must be artificial, and therefore that using them means appealing to intellectual contrivances instead of movement as it exists before our intellect reconstructs it. I have no reason to deny that the units I have mentioned are conceptualized by intellect. But far from lending support to Bergson's position, this only indicates that the experience of movement involves more than his ideas about the intuition of "pure mobility" would allow. I am suggesting that without the operation of our intellect, we would never perceive motion in the way that we normally do.

Bergson invokes the concept of pure mobility because he thinks there *must* be something logically prior to any idea of movement that involves the intellect. But we cannot make sense of pure mobility unless we identify it with continuity. Since continuity is itself a part of what we mean by movement, however, it cannot yield the logical priority Bergson ascribes to pure mobility. The being of continuity enables us to say that movement is experienced as an indivisible totality, but this can only mean that movement is seen to be continuous. Nevertheless, it is also seen as a trajectory in space and time; and that must implicate the contrafactual conditionals I have mentioned.

If one had the leisure, I think one could show that most of Bergson's failings as a metaphysician result from mistakes about continuity. For example, consider his fundamental distinction between duration and spatial time. In duration we have a feeling of uninterrupted movement—the progressive flow of our inner life, as Bergson sometimes calls it—that seems to have no logical connection with space and that can be understood only as continuity itself. In space, and in the time related to space, Bergson argues, continuity never occurs since space and spatial time are divisible and therefore always discontinuous. On both of these points, it seems to me that Bergson has misconstrued the nature of continuity.

When I listen to music, for instance, I do have a sense of movement that is independent of spatial configurations. But this does not signify that I experience nothing but continuity itself. What I hear is a continuity *in* the musical notes, a continuity *in* the pattern of sounds. Instead of contrafactual conditionals involving locations in space and time, I would have to explain this sense of movement in terms of different pitches at different times, or different dynamics at different times, depending on the type of continuity I have in mind. Pure continuity, continuity apart from everything else, I never experience.

On the other hand, I often encounter continuity in space even when there is no movement and even though space is divisible. A static line is both divisible and still continuous unless it has intervals, that is, unless it is a dotted line. A dotted line is discontinuous, an unbroken line is not. Since each of the little lines that make up a dotted line is perfectly continuous, Bergson ought to argue that just as continuity explains pure mobility so too does it explain pure spatiality. He rejects that possibility because he thinks that static lines cannot be continuous in the same sense in which the movement of an object is. But he is surely mistaken about that. In every sense in which a movement is continuous, so too is a line. Movements are movements and lines are lines, and of course they are not the same in every way. But with respect to continuity, I find no difference whatsoever. A movement in time is continuous in not being broken up, and the same is true of a line in space.

Something similar applies when Bergson talks about immediate perception of reality. The faculty of intuition, as he envisages it, largely consists in the ability to detect continuity. Analysis dissociates thing from thing, moment from moment, sensation from sensation; but, Bergson assures us, all being is really a unitary and purely continuous becoming. The true nature of being, he says, is evident in the constant way that life directly impinges upon us. When we strip away the falsifications of the intellect, we find that experience is just a continuous flow of this sort. We then live by intuition alone and commune with reality itself.

Here again, it seems to me that mistaken assumptions about continuity have led Bergson astray. He is right to think that in any sense in which something is directly perceived, continuity is. For instance, if someone claims that the color of this table is directly perceived but that the date of its original manufacture is not, I readily understand him. He means that we just look and see the color but that we have to infer the table's date by getting information about its style, its construction, and so on. In a comparable fashion, continuity is also directly perceived. We just open our eyes and there it is. The continuity is perceived directly, much as a color is. If this were doubted, we might cite experiments by empirical psychologists.

There should not be any question about this much. Difficulties enter only when a philosopher like Bergson fabricates a metaphysical category out of the innocent fact that continuity is experienced with the same immediacy as a color. One inevitably wonders why he believes that continuity is so special in this regard. Even *dis*continuity is directly perceived that way. I do not have to make any inferences in order to see that an interrupted motion or a dotted line is discontinuous. If the criterion is directness of perception, I find nothing in the nature of continuity to warrant the speculative use to which Bergson puts it.

But perhaps there is another criterion. When Bergson talks about intuition, he generally alludes to a sense of interpenetration. The flowing of duration is such, he thinks, that nothing in it appears to consciousness as a discrete entity. Everything belongs to a spectrum of interweaving qualities. As in the chromatic spectrum no single color can be sharply demarcated from its neighbors, so too is reality as a whole thought to consist of interpenetrating feelings, ideas, material processes and events. In opposition to my suggestion that discontinuities are directly perceived, Bergson would argue that we misunderstand the nature of colors, sounds, odors, aches, pains, or other experiential qualities if we think of them as discrete items in our consciousness. Actually, he would say, it is their continuous *flux* that we experience, their interpenetration within the fluid texture of our lives. Inasmuch as discontinuity implies a lack of interpenetration, it can be perceived only indirectly, derivatively, and through the fallible operation of the intellect. The perception of continuity enjoys metaphysical primacy because it alone includes the truthful awareness of interpenetration.

At this point, there are two questions we must ask ourselves. First, does continuity always imply interpenetration? Second, is either continuity or interpenetration a fundamental constant in human experience of the world? Bergson would answer both questions in the affirmative. I myself feel that at least the first question must be answered negatively, even though there are obvious cases where continuity does imply interpenetration. The continuity of the chromatic spectrum is a function of the interpenetration of its regional parts. The same holds for a chain made up of links. But the continuity of a spectrum or a chain is quite different from the continuity of a moving object or an unbroken line. In the latter examples, there is no interpenetration. My hand moves continuously from table to book. It traverses a series of positions in which it might have come to rest but does not. The positions can be chosen in such a way that they overlap and thus interpenetrate one another. But these possible interpenetrations do not explain the *continuity* in movement, for that depends on the fact that I never do stop in any of the relevant spaces. They are only hypothetical. They are not parts of the movement in the sense in which links are parts of a chain or colors parts of a spectrum. Consequently, even if the possible positions would overlap, the continuity in movement is not a function of their interpenetration. Though jointly present on some occasion, continuity and interpenetration are logically independent.

The second question I find more difficult to answer. I am not sure what might count as a "fundamental constant." I do not know exactly what Bergson is looking for. In my experience I discover continuities and discontinuities, interpenetration and the lack of it. How does one decide which is more fundamental? If someone were to claim that a dotted line is "really" continuous, I would be confused at first. But then I might try to make sense of what this person is saying—he or she means that you still see it as a single line, not as a random cluster of little ones. And that is true. My attention is being called to something in my experience that I may not have been fully aware of. If someone else had denied that a dotted line is continuous, however, I would have taken this as stressing the fact that it has intervals. And that too is true.

I find no basis for preferring one of these statements over the other. But I do recognize how each of them might manifest a separate mode of seeing an empirical phenomenon, even leading, perhaps, to different attitudes toward life. The nature of our chosen language in metaphysics or ontology can have importance beyond metaphysics and ontology. For this reason, it seemed to me essential to study Bergson's view of intuition as a prelude to his moral and affective philosophy. Moreover, there is a crucial aspect of Bergsonian intuition that I have not touched on as yet and that comes out most clearly in his ideas about what he calls "sympathetic identification." We are now ready to study those ideas.

Though Bergson sometimes refers to sympathetic identification as "intellectual sympathy," he wishes to distinguish it from the workings of intellect or analysis. It is an intuition through which "one places oneself within an object in order to coincide with what is unique in [that object] and consequently inexpressible."[4] This happens when we identify ourselves with another person, when we share some experience of his or hers. Bergson draws upon ordinary expressions like "seeing someone from the inside," or "putting ourselves in another's position." I have virtually no idea what Bergson means when he speaks of placing oneself within a material object, but I think I do understand him when he talks this way about a possible relationship with other people.

For Bergson, intuition is both feeling and cognition. By identifying with another in the most sympathetic manner possible, he says, we experience a simple, indivisible sense of what that individual is like. Out of such feelings we can derive a great deal of knowledge about the person and his or her reality; without the requisite feeling, the true nature of this individual always eludes us. As distinct from analysis, intuition employs no explicit concepts. Analysis reduces people to elemental properties they have in common with other human beings we have already encountered. It thereby treats them as if they were just members of a class, which is something different from what they are in themselves. That is the usual inadequacy of the intellect. Only intuition enables us to know other people as they really are: persons whose attributes interpenetrate within a continuity of experience that is uniquely their own over and above any extraneous classification, however suitable it may be.

As I have said, this doctrine has importance in Bergson's moral philosophy as well as his metaphysics. He uses it to distinguish between two types of morality: the open and the closed. Closed morality consists of communal mandates operating in a nonpersonal way. It impresses upon each man or woman a sense of identity with the particular group to which he or she belongs. Insofar as our morality is closed, we resemble the social insects. Our actions are controlled by rules the clan or nation has inculcated without consulting us in advance. Since moral commandments are impersonal, they build up habits that eventually speak with the faceless voice of conscience.

Open morality, on the other hand, employs aspiration rather than pressure or a sense of obligation. We are then motivated by a desire to emulate people whose conduct we admire. These role models—saints and heroes—break the bonds of closed morality. They act out of a personal love for humanity. Not being guided by the quasi-instinctual demands of a closed society, they choose to ally themselves with life as it flows on in all human beings. They are the great practitioners of intuition, sympathetically identifying with others, working for their welfare through self-dedication instead of coerced allegiance to any society. Their devotion comes from an experience of mystical oneness, which Bergson describes as an intuitive unity with the God whose essence is love itself. Though Bergson occasionally speaks of the diety as a person, he thinks of God as the creative impulse in nature which propels all existence to further and augmented possibilities of goodness. Open morality is thus grounded in cosmic love that is somehow primordial in the ever-interpenetrating universe. All human beings are said to participate in this love to the extent that their powers of sympathetic identification are properly awakened.[5]

There is a great deal in Bergson's conception of open morality that we might discuss. It would be instructive to compare Bergson on love with C. S. Peirce on agapasm, or Plotinus on eros and Aquinas on caritas. But here I want to concentrate on the role of intuition. I will study it in this context much as I did in discussing the problem about movement. Bergson's approach to morality is similar to his conception of motion. As he remarks that intuitive and analytic ideas of movement occur together in ordinary parlance, so too does he suggest that both types of morality are present in everyday experience. And as he gives metaphysical preference to pure mobility, so too does he extol open morality as the ideal goal toward which human conduct should direct itself.

From the very outset, it seems to me that Bergson is correct in one important respect. In part, at least, his way of distinguishing between open and closed morality is designed to preclude the reduction of the former to the latter. Open morality embodies the ideal of love for humankind in general, and every human being in particular. Closed morality involves concern for the welfare of one's own society, one's own family, one's own people, one's own immediate surroundings. By insisting that these are two different kinds of morality, Bergson rightly emphasizes that there is something in the love of humanity that is different from closed morality.

We can see the significance of this view by comparing Bergson with Hume. Unlike Bergson, Hume bases all morality on a single, innate sentiment of benevolence or sympathy. Hume feels that sympathy for persons remote from us is always much weaker than sympathy for those who are closely related, but he believes that humanitarian love consists in extending toward everyone the type of solicitude we have for intimates. How do we do this? By means of what Hume calls the "judicious intellect." We render our sympathy more extensive, he says, by using the calmness of reflection to rise above indifference that stems from whatever feeling of remoteness that may also exist. We thereby work out principles of morality that apply to all men and women. And although, as Hume maintains, "the heart" is not regulated by these general mandates, he concludes that "being sufficient, at least for discourse, [they] serve all our purposes in company, in the pulpit, on the theatre, and in the schools."[6]

This is the kind of analysis that Bergson rejects. When he says that open morality is not the "extension of an instinct" and does not originate in an idea, when he argues that "social instincts" may possibly account for the love of one's family or country but not for the love of humanity, he has Humean reductivism in mind. In my opinion Bergson's attack is justified. To the degree that he refers to a feeling in the love of humanity which Hume's analysis overlooks, I think he is heading in the right direction. By downplaying any relevant feeling, Hume treats the love of those who are remote from us as a merely intellectual gesture. Indeed, one may wonder why we ever need to feel sympathy at all in order to "love" humanity in the manner Hume describes. He could be talking about the character in Dostoyevsky who says he loves mankind as a whole but admits that there are hardly any people whose presence he can stand.

The love of humanity consists of more than just the disposition to say edifying things on public occasions, or even to act for the sake of philanthropic causes. Whatever its faults may be, Bergson's philosophy recognizes that the love of humanity is not merely an extension of communal instincts in a closed society. It involves a different type of affect.

Where then does Bergson go wrong? I think he errs in his depiction of the irreducible residue in open morality. He portrays sympathetic identification as a means of interpenetrating with the vital continuity in another person and doing so without any reliance on concepts of the intellect. Since the uniqueness of another consists of that much human life that is in him or her, and since the principle of all life is the creative flow in reality as a whole, Bergson concludes that sympathetic identification puts us in rapport with the ultimate nature of Being itself. There is no simple way of testing the validity of this belief. But if we can adequately describe open morality without recourse to the metaphysical faculty Bergson invokes, do we not have good reason to discard his view of moral intuition? For one thing, notice how recklessly he lumps together identification, sympathy, and love. These are quite distinct, not only from each other but also from sentiments like benevolence, compassion, empathy, pity, and respect. To make my point I do not need to examine all of the moral feelings. It will suffice to analyze identification, sympathy, and love; and to consider in each case whether Bergson's ideas about intuition might possibly apply.

❄

I start with identification. We often speak of identifying with other people. Does this mean that we ourselves experience the flow that is unique in those persons? I doubt that. What is unique about a person is merely his being the person he or she happens to be. It is the fact of his or her separate identity. But when we *identify* with another, we do not merge or coincide or interpenetrate with his or her uniqueness, or duplicate, or even re-present it. Those states, which differ from each other, would rob or undermine the individual's identity. Far from replicating any unique continuity, identification implies feeling and behaving that make an attribute in some other person common to oneself and that other person. Through identification people share in another's personhood and even appropriate its reality. In identifying with his father, a son draws from the father certain characteristics that he takes as his own. The son incorporates them in himself. He is severe with his children much as his father was with him, he gets into the habit of drinking a glass of wine during dinner like his father, in diverse situations he acts in ways that are remarkably similar to what his father would have done.

Having acquired those habits, the son may closely resemble the father; and to that extent, one might say that his behavior, and his feelings as well, coincide with those of his father. But that only means that father and son are alike in some respects. It does not mean that the son has interpenetrated the very nature and uniqueness of his father's life. On the contrary, the son has quite literally introduced his father—or rather, his traits—into an area of his own life. Identifying with someone is like adhering to a political cause. If we call ourselves Republicans or Democrats, we announce that there exists in us some of the same network of sentiments and beliefs that are present in other people of this persuasion. We do not merge or interpenetrate with them. Their uniqueness as individuals is not at stake. Bergsonian intuitionism does not help us to understand the situation.

But perhaps it will be said that Bergson was talking about identification of a different kind. What other kind is there? Well, there's putting yourself in the other fellow's shoes, seeing the world from his point of view. These expressions are better approached in terms of sympathy rather than identification. Through sympathy we do put ourselves in someone else's position and see things from his or her point of view, without necessarily appropriating that person's traits. But Bergson would still insist that in sympathy, at least, we enter into another's life directly, without the use of concepts, and thus experience through intuition what is unique about the continuity of that reality.

Take an example. A friend of yours is building a bookcase. His hand slips and the hammer comes down on his thumb. You see the expression on his face; you hear him exclaim "ouch!" What does it mean to say that you feel sympathy for him, that you sympathize? Bergson would call attention to the uniqueness of your friend's pain, which has a location within his ongoing experience and no one else's. Bergson maintains that through sympathy you undergo your friend's reality the way he does himself.

Is this accurate? I do not think so. Regardless of how sympathetic you may be, you generally feel nothing comparable to what your friend has felt. Your friend's thumb hurts, but yours does not. Notice that when your friend makes the exclamation of pain, your response is significantly different. You do not say "ouch!" (or if you do, it is in a wholly special kind of voice—a dramatic intonation reserved for displaying sympathy). You say something like: "That must hurt!"; or you say nothing and go fetch a cold compress.

To put yourself in another's position is not to *feel* what he or she feels, but rather to imagine what that feeling is and to have feelings of your own that evince your concern about his or her condition. That is why it would have been unsympathetic for you to have remarked: "I told you not to use that hammer" or "I was sure you would hurt yourself." In talking like that, you are not expressing sympathy for your friend. He is in pain and wants to have his pain recognized and possibly alleviated. For the moment, he is not interested in how the accident could have been avoided, or that he has only himself to blame for its occurrence. In looking for sympathy, he hopes that you will have a corresponding, but not identical, feeling. There is no question of your feeling what he does.

I detect three components in sympathy, none of which pertains to Bergsonian intuition. First, there is the fact that we attend to what the other person is feeling. Our response coincides with what is unique in him or her only in the sense that it is his or her misfortune that we care about at the time. The actuality we focus on is the same for us as for him, which would not have been the case if we had said: "Look, you've got nothing to complain about. Last week, when *I* hit my thumb . . ." and so on. We would then have been concentrating on our past feeling, not the one the other person has right now.

Second, in reacting sympathetically to someone else's experience, we perceive it in its actual relation to that individual. If he is an old carpenter used to such accidents, his pain does not elicit from us the same reaction as if he were a novice suddenly encountering the perils of hammering. In feeling sympathy toward another, we consider what the event means to *that person*. If we thought the novice preferred that no one knew about his incompetent hammering, sympathy might require us to say little, if anything, about his pain and to do nothing about lessening it.

Finally, and perhaps this sums up what I have been suggesting, sympathy means that what matters to the other man or woman matters to oneself not for its own sake but because of its importance to him or her. You may be hardened to pain. In itself its occurrence may scarcely give you pause. But if you are sympathetic, it will matter to you as something that another cares about, albeit from a different point of view.

To change the example, imagine that a friend of yours wants to make a lot of money. It may not matter to you that he should succeed in this desire. In fact you might think that it would be very bad for him. But if you are sympathetic, what does matter is the fact that it is what he wants—it matters to *him*. Your total involvement is not at all the same as his, but only geared and relevant to it. In some respects, your response might be proportionate. The value you bestow upon your friend's craving could be commensurate to the importance he accords it himself. If you treat his ambition, or his pain in the previous illustration, more seriously than he does, your concern seems overly solicitous and you run the risk of aggressing against his personal autonomy. If you treat his attitude or experience less seriously than he does, you are, to that extent, indifferent.

As it normally exists, sympathy is a highly complex disposition consisting of both intellect and feeling. Bergson does well to say that it enables us to understand another person in his or her unique individuality. But this we do by a special use of concepts, not by their elimination. Through sympathy we resonate both cognitively and affectively to the feelings and desires of others, and by appreciating the role they have for *them*, as whatever persons they are. Bergson recognizes that this is not the same as just observing the man or woman's plight scientifically, as a quantifiable datum, or as something to be explained by reference to general principles within which it may be subsumed. But Bergson mistakenly concludes that the sympathetic attitude is completely nonanalytic.

Instead, we should infer that sympathy is incompatible only with *detached* analysis. In sympathy we attach our analysis to the person being analyzed, and we also attach ourselves inasmuch as we take a personal interest in him or her that differs from mere observation. These unifying efforts take us beyond the intellect in isolation, but they do not negate it or imply Bergsonian intuition. They are modes of affective involvement that can occur in various life situations. Sympathy converts them into felt concern that may sometimes eventuate as love or compassion.

Identification (or empathy, as it is also called) may often exist without inducing much if any feelings of benevolence, but sympathy embodies the latter within itself. Whatever I may do or say, I am at least sorry that my friend is in pain. Sympathy differs from compassion in not requiring that my feelings issue into consecutive action, but nevertheless my having sympathy shows that I have a good will toward the other person. I will be pained that he should be in pain, though I will not be *in* pain myself. I will care about what he cares about, not only in giving it parallel and proportionate significance but also in feeling that if I can I *ought* to help him in his hour of need.

This is not to deny that the term *sympathy*, or some modification of it, is sometimes used in cases where benevolent feelings are totally lacking. A gifted general who can sense what is going on in his adversary's mind—who can anticipate his enemy's moves without amassing detailed evidence—may be said to do so by "sympathetic attunement." Usually, however, sympathy is taken to entail a positive interest in the welfare of the other. The general's talent is more properly described as a capacity to put himself in some other person's position. He will use this aptitude to sympathize with his friends, but he will show no sympathy for those he wishes to destroy. Toward the latter he doubtless feels nothing that is related to love of them as human beings.

Consequently, if the love of humanity can be understood as either identification or (benevolent) sympathy, it is the second of these that has the greatest explanatory value. Identification may serve as a causal condition for sympathy, compassion, or love to exist. But since it itself need not involve benevolence, identification can hardly elucidate these other dispositions. Nor should we rely upon any mystical faculty of intuition. We do better to look for more plausible ways of combining observable feelings and appropriate concepts. In doing so, we can readily agree with Hume (and Freud) that sympathy and compassion are usually limited to members of our own social group. But then, wherein consists the love of humanity? And how can we effect the distinction between open and closed morality, as Bergson cogently demands?

In searching for a type of feeling that is different from abstract judgment but still has the universal scope implied by the love of humankind, perhaps we do well to consider the conditions under which sympathy and compassion normally appear. Think again about our earlier example. It was easy to imagine what the man who hammered his thumb was going through. We have all had comparable experiences: we often hurt ourselves by accident. And yet we may also sympathize with people whose lives are extremely different from ours. If we saw a photograph of a woman tearfully watching her home burn down, we might surely sympathize, even though we ourselves have never been in that situation. Of course, at one time or another we too have lost something we cherished, but the fact remains that in sympathizing with this person we are conscious of differences between our experiences whereas in sympathizing with our carpenter friend we draw upon similarities.

This gives us the key to what we want to know. In closed morality, we sympathize with people who are like ourselves. Sympathy is then furthered by the tightness of our social relations, by the many aspects in which living together causes us to have the same kind of existence. In open morality, we move beyond the groups to which we belong and sympathize with people who are not at all similar to us. Different as these people may be, however, they are human beings we see as persons, as we see ourselves. In closed morality, we sympathize with social intimates, with men and women who resemble us in their origins, their cultural backgrounds, their allegiances, their interests, and their beliefs. In open morality, we sympathize with others merely because they are human. We sympathize with them *as persons*, regardless of the many ways in which their lives are alien to our own.

The love of humanity thus includes a particular kind of sympathy, but one that is sufficiently common to be interesting for ethical theory. I use the word *includes* because I do not think that sympathy is ever a sufficient condition for people to love each other. Love goes beyond sympathy in creating a pervasive and sometimes permanent attachment. Love bestows panoramic value: it accepts someone despite his or her faults and imperfections. Love often shows itself in sympathy, and we can imagine circumstances in which we would deny that a person did love someone else if he or she had no sympathy toward that other person. But though love and sympathy are related, they also diverge.

For one thing, there are different types of interpersonal love, and sympathy is not present or alike in all of them. There are differences between a mother's love and the love of humanity. The mother loves her infant as a separate being who is also an extension of herself. Her love depends on a bond that is directly physical as well as social. To love humanity, however, is to be disposed toward others regardless of their remoteness or lack of intimacy in both respects. It is an ability to accept people as just the persons they are even though we have little in common with them. The love of persons may exist in closed relations—between husband and wife, for instance, or between friends—but it becomes the love of humanity only when it manifests the capacity to bestow value upon others *simply* because they are human beings. In that event we are prepared to love them indiscriminately, not only as the particularity that each of them is but also regardless of the fact that we may not know the nature of their particular attributes.

In the closed society we do not love indiscriminately. Our positive feeling, our attachment, our benevolent attitude— in short, our bestowal of value—is parceled out to members of our group. Other creatures, including those that are also human, remain excluded from our concern. We treat them as conveniences or even prey that nature has provided for the benefit of ourselves and our social cohorts. The basis of this response may well be instinctual in ways that sociobiologists or other scientists may yet discern. Bergson anticipates their work in his speculative philosophy. He suggests that inherited patterns within our affective instincts may explain why the closed society is ridden with class divisions and hierarchical orderings that determine who in the group is considered an "insider" supremely worthy of loving attention, and who is not. Be this as it may, Bergson is wrong to think that *indiscriminate* sympathy does not come from the same cauldron. It too originates in the closed society, however much it may transcend it.

To account for the love of humanity we must therefore discover the vectors within our natural constitution which Bergson ignores. Hume recommends the dispassionate operation of intellect because he thinks that it forces us to see that all people are alike as participants in the human race. And it is true that this awareness can open up the closed society. It encourages us to extend toward those who are outside whatever pale has been established by some group the same caring attitude bestowed upon the insiders. But in making his suggestion, Hume minimizes the affective dimension in the love of humanity. Bergson perceives, more clearly than he does, that affirmative feelings may also be at work. Bergson's error consists in thinking that intuition as he conceives of it elucidates those feelings.

If I am right, we can define the open society without any reference to Bergsonian intuition. The love of humanity is indeed a feeling, and sympathy of a sort contributes to it. But once we recognize that there are different types of sympathy, as there are different types of love, we can distinguish between the closed and the open society along those lines. Sympathy toward our intimates or fellows in a circumscribed group is an extension of our own self-love. Other people are then treated either like ourselves in ways we cherish or else as collaborative agents in enterprises that further our joint interests. Our sympathy, and whatever love is related to it, devolves from the realization that our urgent needs can be satisfied better in association with these individuals than if we remained detached from them. Gregarious feeling, which is so powerful in the closed society, is based on a kind of selfishness that everyone in a group can experience simultaneously and to the mutual advantage of all the others in that group.

Were this the only kind of sympathy, there would be no love of humanity and no open society. We transcend the boundaries of the closed society by cultivating another mode of sympathetic response. It is less self-oriented insofar as we ourselves may benefit only slightly from it. Our sympathy for starving children in some distant region of Africa may not have much effect upon our personal well-being. All the same, our philanthropic sentiment, as distinct from the dispassionate judgment Hume describes, is deeply embedded in our condition as human beings. Without greatly identifying with the African children or thinking that we will ever be in their position, we cannot fail to recognize their metaphoric kinship to us and to those about us whom we love more intimately. If we have a love of humanity, we extend the sympathy we feel toward associates, friends, and family to people we will never meet or know in person. When that happens, the nature of the sympathy changes but it is still a feeling as well as being a product of the intellect. In becoming indiscriminate, or rather less discriminate, it remains an affective as well as judgmental response.

The nature of the different feelings that comprise either closed or open sympathy may be classified in relation to alternate modes of imagination. More than intellect is needed for the choice of objects toward which we have sympathy of any kind. Even a humane person may feel little distress about a famine in Africa until he or she sees on the television screen an image of some starving child. Just knowing about such catastrophes is often not enough to create a moral sentiment in us. Our heart is touched, as we say, by the *spectacle* of innocent children being forced to suffer. The picture activates our imagination; it shows and reminds us of misery that can descend upon human beings anywhere and at any time. In the closed society, imagination is differently directed; we contemplate a different spectrum of possibilities, most of which reflect the dimensions of life we have known as members of a group. In both cases imagination works in tandem with judgments and idealizations afforded through the intellect. Whatever sympathy issues forth results from the varied interplay between imagination and intellect.

Distinctions between the closed and open society can be very useful in moral philosophy. Conclusions in both fields of interest have their ties to the innate structures we have been discussing, and neither field requires Bergsonian-type intuition. Identification is a factor, since sympathy presupposes at least some degree of empathy. How else could we know who is or is not a human being like ourselves? Empathy is not enough to explain either the love of humanity or the open society in general. Yet neither is sympathy sufficient unto itself. It too must be supplemented by compassion as a proactive response that causes us to delight in the possibility of happiness that others might experience, and, as a consequence, to take their sufferings upon ourselves. In a closed society these other people may be only our compatriots, but even then we supplement our sympathetic feelings with behavior that seeks to increase their well-being through our compassionate response. In a truly open society any human being qualifies as a candidate for compassion as well as sympathy, for moral action on our part as the explicit expression of what we feel. An authentic love of humanity depends on both.

❆

I suggest, therefore, that the irreducible residue in open morality is a kind of sympathy and compassionate love that goes beyond the limitations of one's social group. It is a form of feeling, not just a demonstration of judiciousness, and it is directed toward individuals rather than an abstract genus. But it would seem to be quite different from what Bergson calls sympathetic identification.

Bergson's approach to this problem is vitiated by philosophical defects similar to those that accompanied his conception of movement. As in the case of pure mobility, he accords open morality a kind of logical priority that seems wholly unwarranted. Love of humanity is a part of morality, but it is not a direction in which true morality must or should tend to the exclusion of everything else. In effect, that is what Bergson advocates. He thinks ethical progress involves the gradual elimination of closed morality. Is this what we really want? Would we not prefer a world order in which local affiliations and broadly humanitarian attitudes conflicted as little as possible? The open and the closed are both essential for the enlarged morality to which most of us subscribe.

This harmonization is embodied in the ideal of the "brotherhood of man." Brotherhood is a closed relation of family intimacy and biological affinity. The ideal consists in extending it to all human beings, including women as well as men, of course. In point of fact, a complete extension can never be carried out, and that is why open morality cannot be reduced to closed morality even in principle. A closed society is surely attainable; an open society can only be approximated, since unknown—and even unknowable—individuals may always elude our limited imagination. But as long as the two types of morality remain in a viable interaction with each other, we have no reason to sacrifice or subordinate either of them.

As this point we can now return to the Bergsonian notion of continuity and interpenetration which I discussed in the first part of this chapter. The practical intent of Bergson's philosophy is to encourage us to employ these concepts, as he interprets them, for understanding the world and envisaging the good life. My doubts about his proposal spring from my belief that discontinuity and lack of interpenetration are also deeply rooted in our reality. Even sympathy and compassion, which are means of effecting spiritual unity, require indefeasible separateness in a way that Bergson does not recognize.

Compared with the sensitivity to differences among human dispositions which one finds in Proust (just to mention a thinker who belongs to the same tradition), Bergson's writing seems primitive, simpleminded, monomelodic.[7] His talent consists in creating an integrated doctrine based on his conception of intuition as the key to continuity and interpenetration. Twenty-first-century thinkers will be satisfied with his general approach only if they have faith in his use of these ideas. To the extent that they do not, as I do not, they will feel a need to construct their modern philosophical edifice with other building blocks.[8]

8

Ortega on Love

As Ecclesiastes might have said: Of the making of love there is no end. Yet love as an ideal condition, and therefore different from the mere pursuit of it, may be less common than many people think. If it is what moves the universe, as Dante claimed, it must do so in strange and mysterious ways. Perhaps that is why novelists have made it their stock-in-trade and scientists tend to ignore it. Published in English about forty-five years ago, José Ortega y Gasset's *Estudios sobre el amor* was one of the few books by a professional philosopher at that time to deal with the subject.[1] It is a fascinating little book—in fact, too fascinating, for it is the kind that gets scorned by *les hommes sérieux*. Yet in its diffuse and aimless way perhaps it does more than a lengthy treatise might have.

Ever since Plato spoke of love as "a desire for generation and birth in beauty," philosophers have often defined love as one kind of desire or another. Ortega mentions Aquinas, who speaks of love as the desire for something good insofar as it is good. He could also have cited Freud, for whom love is fundamentally desire for anything insofar as it is sexual.

There is something strange about this manner of defining love. It is as if a visitor to earth had asked you what movies look like and instead of telling him about images darting across the screen you showed him a reel of film. Of course there is a close connection between the movies and the film. Scientists explain the connection when they talk about the stroboscopic effect. But movies are movies and film is film. As a great philosophical simpleton once said: Everything is what it is and not another thing. Love is what it is; it is not desire, which is another thing.

Ortega sees this. He strenuously insists that sentiments like love and hate must not be confused with desires or appetites. He argues that love is usually followed by desire, for instance the desire for sexual union, but that desire can exist without love (the addict desires drugs while also hating them). Moreover, Ortega thinks that love can occur in its purity prior to any desire. To desire something is to want to possess it, to incorporate it within oneself; but, Ortega says, to love is to forgo possession and make oneself a part of the beloved.

Thus love is not reducible to desire. But shall we say that desire is a mere consequence of love, an accompaniment that in no way constitutes its being? I think not. Ortega goes too far. In his eagerness to escape the confusion between affect and appetite, he acts as if each can be defined entirely apart from the other. When he speaks of sexual desire as being different from love, he remarks that our sexuality can be satisfied by any number of objects whereas love is very selective. He also maintains that "nine-tenths of that which is attributed to sexuality is the work of our magnificent ability to imagine, which is no longer an instinct, but exactly the opposite: . . . a specifically human creation—like literature. In both, the most important factor is imagination."[2] But if this is so, as I believe it to be, perhaps the selectivity of love and the relative promiscuity of sex are more closely related than Ortega allows. Imagination is the key to both.

Lust sometimes appears when love has been stymied. The man who cannot love any woman may seek to recoup his loss by going through "the act of love" with a succession of women. Since his desire arose out of an inability to love, he will probably use his erotic imagination as a means of dominating them all. On the other hand, an accomplished lover may find it essential to do with a special woman what he knows that he can do with any other. Love is expressed by the imaginative act of deploying our sexuality in relation to someone we care about. It is because they know that all women like flowers that each of them is flattered when a man sends bouquets only to her.

Desire is therefore a part of love, not something separate or a mere consequence of it. To desire is not necessarily to love; but to love is *at least* to desire. The lover desires the permanent happiness of the beloved; the parent desires what is good for the child; the friend desires the welfare of his or her buddy. In each case, one's love means making the other a part of oneself as well as making oneself a part of this different person. The lover's desire can succeed only if it furthers intimate contact with the beloved, the parent's only if it contributes to the rearing of the child, the friend's only if it conduces to a life together at the same time as it enforces an appropriate distance. A good deal of love consists in the desire to be what the beloved is, and in that sense to incorporate the beloved within oneself. This is particularly evident in love within a single gender, but it applies to all forms of intimacy. The brusque young man is drawn to the graceful lady by his longing to be like her, in his own way to be graceful himself.

❄

Having told us what love is not, Ortega tries to give a definition of his own. But each time he makes that effort, the delineation changes greatly. A collection of essays written at different times, the book is subtitled "Aspects of a Single Theme." I am not sure what that theme could be. Certainly it is not a univocal way of characterizing love. Moving from one of Ortega's formulations to another is like watching Picasso paint in the film *Le Mystère Picasso*. Version succeeds version with astounding rapidity, sometimes getting better, sometimes worse. One eventually feels a critic's impulse to narrow this flow of brilliant, but often damaging, improvisation; one wants to shout at the artist to stop, to leave things alone, not to fiddle any more. But with relentless fertility the ideas multiply and disperse. These masters are also sorcerer's apprentices, albeit of the highest order, artists in the service of teeming virtuosity rather than good taste.

I will not try to enumerate Ortega's different definitions. Some of them may not be definitions at all. Ortega often throws us off by acting as if his statements are literal and all-inclusive when they are really designed to add a bit of extra, but dispensable, coloration—somewhat like an answer to the question "What is a Communist?" that I read in a magazine some time ago: "A Communist is a dirty rat." In this vein Ortega says that love is "a centrifugal act of the soul in constant flux that goes towards the object and envelops it in warm corroboration, uniting us with it and positively affirming its being."[3] The suggestion that love is a kind of affirmation is intriguing. I will return to it later. As for the rest of Ortega's statement, which sounds a little like a description of central heating, I pass it over in respectful silence.

In another place Ortega says it is "essential for true love to be born suddenly and never to die."[4] ("Love is not love which alters when it alteration finds"?) He, and Shakespeare, may be right. But I can't help feeling like the skeptical little boy who, coming upon a copy of Kipling's *Just So Stories* and scrutinizing the title, remarked: "Well, I doubt it." I feel that way too when I read that love is "eternally unsatisfied."[5] My reaction is: He's not talking about men and women in love; he's talking about "swains" or something like that.

Some of the other formulations are more persuasive and warrant more careful treatment. Consider the idea that to be in love is "to continually and intentionally give life to *something which depends upon us*. Loving is perennial vivification, creation and *intentional* preservation of what is loved."[6] I find this very hard to accept. To give life to something, to create it, to make it depend upon us is not to love it. Loving involves accepting someone as an independent being. What we create may have life, like the infant that has just been pushed on stage, but it does not yet have a life of its own. It attains that once it has emancipated itself from the dependency of creation. Only then, or with that as a prospect of its future autonomy, is it capable of loving and being loved.

There is nothing surprising in the fact that parents and children find it difficult to love each other. For the parents this means accepting the children as separate individuals capable of independent development. But that seems to negate the fact that the child is the parent's offspring, his or her creation. For their part, children are often embarrassed at the necessity of loving parents they never chose, about whom they weren't even consulted. "I didn't ask to be born," meaning "I didn't ask to be born to *you*." One of the basic assumptions in *Genesis* is that man should love God because God is his creator. I have never been able to see why. Nor is there any guarantee of God's love in the mere fact of creation, even continual creation. Perhaps God no longer exists for us as once he did because humankind has become more demanding in its search for love.

Similarly, I fail to share Ortega's acceptance of the Platonic doctrine that erotic love culminates in a desire "to leave, as testimony of the union, a child in whom the perfections of the beloved are perpetuated and affirmed."[7] Children are not engendered as testimonials of a loving union, though they may be conceived in the hope that the lovers will strengthen their relationship as a by-product of the joys and challenges that result from having progeny. Love is itself an affirmation of the beloved; from this viewpoint, procreation is supererogation.

Whatever else they may signify, children are made in an act of joint creativity. Parents create for the same reason artists do: as a means of expressing themselves by what they do and to develop aptitudes that otherwise, without their collaboration, might have remained unrealized. Where there is love between the parents, neither has a need to duplicate the being of the beloved. In fact, if Daddy wants a little girl just like Mommy, it seems likely that Daddy is dissatisfied with Mommy as she is. Not loving her as an adult, he absurdly thinks she might be more attractive as a little child. The genuine lover accepts the beloved as he or she is and does not seek to make another person as a living mausoleum of him or her.

In speaking just now of resemblances between the parent and the artist, I did not wish to minimize the differences, which are equally striking. It seems unlikely, though also true to human nature, when Proust says that he wanted his novels published just as a loving parent would want his children to succeed in the world. Artists cannot love their production in the way that parents may come to love a son or daughter. Works of art are inanimate. That is part of their allure. Each audience will interpret them differently, but they themselves have no capacity to develop beyond whatever life the artist has expressed through them. If a sculptor loves his statue, as Pygmalion loved the beautiful Galatea, it is probably himself, his own aesthetic potency, that the man is enamored of.

Perhaps it is not irrelevant that in one version of the myth Pygmalion is a misogynist, and that in another he makes his statue as a pious gift to Aphrodite, who has thwarted his impulse to love by refusing to let him lie with her. In this connection, I see the point in Plato's idea that it is nobler to create people rather than inanimate objects. If you limit yourself to the creation of things, your love runs the risk of being largely narcissistic.

Thus far I have said little about Ortega's conception of love as affirmation. He says little about it himself. He states that love is "a cordial, affirmative interest in another person for himself."[8] In one excellent passage he writes: "[Love] is involved in the affirmation of its object. Think of what it is to love art or your country: it consists of never doubting for an instant their right to exist; it is like recognizing and confirming at each moment that they are worthy of existence. This, not in the manner of a judge who coldly passes a sentence in recognition of a right, but in such a way that the favorable decision is, at the same time, participation in and enactment of that right."[9]

This seems to me to be the right track. If only Ortega had stayed on it! Instead, he loses heart and falls back on Platonism, like so many other theorists. In trying to explain what the lover does affirm, the nature of his choice in love, Ortega tells us it is always the beauty of the beloved. Plato had said the same except that Ortega, addressing a Western rather than a Greek audience, feels he must emphasize that true beauty is not physical but spiritual. As he sees it, love is adherence to a type of humanity considered best; it is "a decision on a certain type of human being, symbolically presented in the details of the face, voice and gestures."[10]

In effect, this position duplicates that of Aquinas. The category of desire has been dropped but there is the same concern for something good insofar as it is good. In other words, there is the same identification of loving and appraising. This, in my opinion, is the greatest mistake of all. Everyone is impelled toward what is good; and certainly we could not love another unless there were something we desired or admired about this person. But love goes beyond that kind of valuation. It is idealization of a different sort. To appraise something is to reach a decision about the goodness of the object. Our judgment often, though not always, purports to be objective. Hamlet may be right when he says that nothing is good or bad but thinking makes it so; yet this does not diminish the fact that we usually think of the goodness or badness as belonging to the object itself.

When love occurs, the situation is quite different. Loving is more than detecting a prior value in the beloved. Love is not just a decision about worth or beauty. It is a way of acting *as if* the beloved were infinitely valuable, which is to say, love is not primarily concerned about actual goodness or badness. Love is to appraisal as imagination is to reality. Like imagination, love does something to its object. It does not create it. It does not make it dependent. It does not change it to suit oneself. It accepts it as it is; but in doing so, it creatively affirms the importance of what it is.

The affirmation in which love consists is neither the recognition of a right nor the perception of a quality. In addition to being appraisive, it is a bestowal of value. It is even the bestowing of a courtesy—*cortesía*, reminiscent of medieval courtliness. As the troubadours knew, love acts as if the lady of one's choice attains perfection merely in being herself. Since, as this world goes, and as everyone knows, perfection generally lies beyond our capacity, the lover bestows upon the beloved something he could never have found in her: the infinite goodness of being treated as what she is not, at the same time as she is accepted as whatever she happens to be. This acceptance bestows an imagined, but not illusory, figment of perfection. To the lover the beloved is both Aphrodite and her own mortal self.

That love is not merely appraisal becomes clear once we consider the difference between stating that something is not good or beautiful and stating that it cannot be loved. There are many things that, in many respects, are neither good nor beautiful. But is anything completely incapable of being loved by someone, sometime, somehow? People in the West have often said that God is love, meaning that he loves everything. Would they say that he finds it all beautiful? Probably not.

Consider the connoisseur who exclaims to a spectator: "How can you like that painting? Its colors are so monotonous." He is providing a reason for finding the painting unaesthetic. But there is no comparable reason to be adduced in matters of love. A mother may say to her son: "How can you love that woman? She's so plain." Is that a good reason for not loving someone? No, it is not.

Nor is this so because love pertains to spiritual rather than physical beauty. It would not help for the young man to reply: "Ah, she has such a good heart." Such an answer indicates he has made the same confusion as his critic and has already jeopardized his right to love. If he were acting in good faith, he would have to renounce his beloved once his mother starts pointing out other faults in the lady. Though they may be relevant to the possibility of enduring or successful love, they cannot prove that one person should not love another.

In the scale of appraisive valuation, we fully accept only the best. In the scale of love, we treat as best what we accept. This does not mean that love involves a dissolution of standards, as some Romantics assumed in thinking that love of life meant subjecting oneself indiscriminately to every kind of amatory experience. In accepting the beloved, the lover may want him or her to attain the greatest good that he or she can. In fact, happiness in love, the fragile condition that lovers always hope to achieve, requires a mutual concern for self-improvement. This cannot occur if one blindly cherishes the other's defects.

In *The Art of Loving*, Erich Fromm distinguishes between mother's love and father's love, the former being an acceptance under any circumstances, the latter involving criteria of better and worse. I think Fromm's labels are misleading since "mother's love" is not limited to mothers, in whom it is often lacking, and "father's love" may only be morality or ambition rather than love itself.

Nevertheless it is useful to think of love in terms of the two heads in a traditional family. Just as the satisfying union between mother and father is necessary for a stable household, so too does adequate love depend upon a viable harmonization of both accepting another and being able to appraise his or her flaws for the sake of eliminating them.

Of course, it is also possible to love a person who really is good or beautiful. And certainly the superiority of the beloved makes it *easier* for love to exist. But this is a causal factor; it does not explain the nature of love. We may love a woman *because* she has good looks, a good figure, a good heart, and a good mind—we love her because of these attributes, we do not love her *for them alone*. If our ability to love were great enough, we would not mind the absence of these qualities.

Love is freely given; it bloweth where it listeth. This is seen more clearly by Cervantes than by Ortega. Don Quixote is not wholly or consistently mad. When the wind is southerly, he knows a hawk from a handsaw better than most men. In a couple of places he recognizes that his beloved Dulcinea del Toboso is really the peasant wench Aldonza Lorenzo. Far from lessening his chivalric love, this awareness intensifies it. As he says, he "contemplate[s] her as she needs must be." He sees her under the aspect of his imagination. The less lovable she may seem, the more his feat of loving her shows that the ways of love are not those of the calculating commonsensical world.

Madness appears in the experience of people like Don Quixote when this feat becomes exclusive and the reality of their Aldonza has scarcely any place in it, as if they thought one can illustrate the fact of gravity by jumping from a tower. It is not in dignifying the woman through his love that the don's insanity consists.

Indeed, we are likely to be suspicious of men or women who love only distinguished and talented persons. It is as if they bestowed upon their beloved what he or she already has. This often happens in people without imagination who swoon before celebrities, like tourists deeply impressed by a monument because it gets three stars in the guide book. In another age the objects of devotion were dashing soldiers or lovely princesses. In our time they more often fall within the class of male and female entertainers. The bestowing that defines this kind of infatuation is derivative from what everyone else thinks. It is dependent on the prominence and the visibility of these individuals—their sheer publicity. Ardent admirers think they love a star of stage, screen, or Internet because their feelings are so greatly aroused. Without knowing it, they are in love with the systems of art and technology that hide from view the reality of this person, even if they partly coincide with what he or she is in fact.

There is no disputing about love, which may be why no two people agree about its suitable recipients. When the Duchesse de Guermantes laments the fact that Swann should have fallen for so inferior a creature as Odette, Proust comments: "It is as if one would be surprised that a patient should deign to undergo cholera given him by so petty a thing as a bacillus."[11] What galls the Duchesse, in my opinion, is not the lowly status of Odette but rather Swann's failure to have consulted her about the advisability of falling in love with this woman. But how could he have? Love is private; only appraisal is public.

Lovers are, in Sartre's words, "seuls au monde" because their condition issues from bestowals that can hardly be communicated to the outsiders. It is the sense of being an outsider to this private oneness that offends a puritan like the Duchesse de Guermantes more than anything else. Society is rendered uneasy by these eddies of isolated imagination that leave the mainstream and dally along the shore. Whence the institution of marriage, which is a public event requiring official documents and a communal ceremony. The wedding ring is not a sign of bondage to the spouse. It is a display of allegiance to social expectations.

While insisting upon the differences between loving and appraisively evaluating, we must also recognize the closeness of their relation. Love is variation on the theme of appraisal. Without appraisal love turns into lust alone, which is another world entirely. Where love plays out the imaginative possibility of perfection, unadulterated lust is simply oblivious to moral or aesthetic value.

I don't think it is a question of love being active while submission to sexual drive is passive, as Ortega says, following the grand tradition of Western philosophy. I think the main difference lies in the fact that in itself lust is scarcely concerned about the possible beauty or goodness of its object. It wants what it wants as a way of satisfying an imperious drive, without introducing questions of worth. While love is stereoscopic and ambles toward its object by shuttling between factuality and imagination, lust makes a beeline for its goal. It can't wait, just as a wild animal can't. There is something pleasantly civilized about "love for wine, women, and song"; there is something brutish about "lust for wine, women, and song." Women recoil from a man who "loves" them merely with a burning need. They rightly sense the contradiction. Men who cultivate that kind of love, and no other, prefer it because they think it increases their power over the female.

Because Ortega misconstrues the relation between love and appraisal his attack on Stendhal lacks much of the force it might have had. Ortega argues that crystallization, as Stendhal conceives of it, cannot clarify the nature of love. Stendhalian crystallization involves illusion, self-deception, he says, whereas love does not. In presenting his case, Ortega distinguishes between being in love and falling in love. He speaks of falling in love as inferior to authentic love, since the former is only a violent and frantic substitute for the latter. He claims that Stendhal confused the one with the other, that he described falling in love but thought he was talking about being in love.

In all this, Ortega's discussion is brilliant, particularly his analysis of falling in love as a phenomenon of attention similar to self-hypnosis. What I find lacking is a last full measure of devotion that might have made sense out of Stendhal. When I look back at De l'Amour and try to see what Ortega has missed, I discover that his very kinship with Stendhal has eluded him. This is what throws him off. Notice the words in which Stendhal defines crystallization: "I call crystallization that process of the mind which discovers fresh perfections in its beloved at every turn of events."[12] Ortega might have said the same himself. It is only the idea that crystallization may be illusory that annoys him. He too believes that love is the search and discovery of perfections.

Given this much agreement, just how penetrating is Ortega's criticism of Stendhal? It is as if they were talking about different, though compatible, aspects of the same thing, each writing in a way that prevents him from seeing what love is like in its totality. Stendhal is impressed by the play of imagination and the lover's tendency to treat his beloved as something better than she is. When the truth begins to seep through the affective marsh, which is the mind of the Stendhalian lover, he falls out of love until such time as his imagination can recharge itself. *That* is not love, Ortega says, and he is right. But he is right for the wrong reasons.

Stendhal's mistake consists in failing to realize fully that we can act as if something is the case even though we know it is not. The lover bestows perfection upon the beloved in *treating* her as if she were perfect; he does not take leave of his senses (except in special cases, more relevant to falling in love rather than being in love). Treating someone the way everyone would like to be treated does not mean living in illusion. Ortega understands this aspect of love. But he takes it to mean that love "has its psychic source in the qualities of the beloved."[13] Not only is this false, since love originates in the lover's need to love, as Stendhal keenly recognized, but also it opens Ortega's position to healthy Stendhalian skepticism.

Ortega asserts that love is too pervasive and fundamental to be based on error. Stendhal would shrug his shoulders. "Why not?" he would reply: "People deceive themselves, all things change, every human relationship is unstable." Perhaps what Ortega calls authentic love, he would assert, does not exist—only boredom and falling in love. This kind of doubt is honest and fairly argued, though in Stendhal accompanied by a compensatory swagger. I am not convinced that Ortega has a satisfactory answer.

Even so, I think that if Stendhal is right he also is right for the wrong reasons. Just because the lover can always have fallacious beliefs about the beloved it does not follow that love is inherently illusory. Love is not a way of making discoveries and therefore it cannot be defined as a making of mistakes. In every human relationship—hatred, indifference, or disgust as well as love—there are discoveries and there are mistakes. But the different attitudes themselves cannot be reduced to any of them. If Stendhal insists that love is a disposition that gives rise to errors of judgment, I assume he is talking about the phenomenon of falling in love, which is only one type of love. And even in this case, what is true—or rather, sometimes true—of falling in love may be equally true of losing one's temper, feeling overwhelming pride, bursting with hatred, and most other strong emotions.

The debate between Ortega and Stendhal is complicated by the fact that in one place, at least, Ortega seems to accept the doctrine he has so vigorously attacked elsewhere. In the last essay in his book, just a hundred pages after Stendhal has been dismissed as "a man who never truly loved nor, above all, was ever truly loved," we find Ortega saying the following: "Romantic love—which is, in my opinion, the prototype and summit of all eroticisms—is characterized by its simultaneously possessing these two ingredients: a feeling of being 'enchanted' by another being who produces complete 'illusion' in us, and a feeling of being absorbed by him to the core of our being. . . . A person in love feels himself totally surrendered to the one he loves."[14] Since Ortega does little to illuminate his use of the words *enchanted* and *illusion*, I can only stand in amazement at this apparent capitulation to the Stendhalian heresy.[15]

The second idea in Ortega's statement, that of letting oneself be absorbed by the beloved, is interesting as a further characterization of love. Ortega speaks pointedly about the "unwilled surrender" that the lover feels. What he says is insightful, I think, and serves to highlight the importance of grace in every affective relationship, not just religious love.

The ability to get what one wants by, in a sense and in a particular manner, no longer wanting it is a talent without which love could not exist. We learn how to love by learning how to devote ourselves, not out of submission or self-abnegation but with faith in the sustaining presence of the beloved, not quietistically but with a sense of adventure. I think of the pilot in David Lean's film *Breaking the Sound Barrier* who magically exceeds the speed of sound by suddenly reversing the controls. I also think of Julien Sorel in Stendhal's *The Red and the Black*, who cannot succeed with Madame de Rênal until he bursts into tears and spontaneously gives up his plans for seducing her.

Ortega's comments on love are sharpened by many a challenging remark about men and women and their relations with each other. For me these aperçus are interesting less as commentary upon human nature than as reflections of the Spanish soul. When Ortega says that every woman presents to the public a conventional, impersonal mask but lives her real life in the recesses of her privacy, I see ladies on a trellised balcony, their suggestive glances obscured by mantillas and silken fans. When he says that every man lives for the sake of public appearances and theatrical demonstrations, I see the matador baring his breast to the bull and offering his heart to the ladies. Ortega remarks that women are by nature irrational and this is what endears them to man, the rational being; that women are a retrogressive force in human selection, choosing to mate with mediocrities instead of the superior males that men generally wish to emulate; that living instinctively means, for women, denial of oneself, for men, the possession of others—particularly the women; that men are restless because of superabundant imagination, whereas women have superior understanding of realities but are generally deficient in imagination.

How are we to take these brave but long since scorned and outmoded generalizations? I feel they have something in common with bullfighting and Spanish dancing, though I am not sure what exactly. Perhaps it is a dualism between body and soul that has been typically Spanish. In no other culture does one find the same attempt to reconcile extremes of spirit and matter, of idealism and realism, of religiosity and worldliness, of civilization and brutality. The matador's art is one of delicacy and creative finesse; yet it is the art of a butcher. The Spanish dancer wears a long formal gown and keeps her torso rigid; but her feet beat out a dionysian rhythm that her upper half pretends to ignore.

Given this Iberian kind of dualism, originating in Manicheanism perhaps, it is not surprising that Ortega should divide the sexes as he does. Despite his desire to open Spanish thinking to the wider currents of European culture, it is primarily as a traditional Spaniard that he himself thinks. I don't condemn this in him; but neither do I wish to overlook it. It is his residual character as a Spaniard that makes him say in the very first sentence of the book: "Let us begin by talking about love, but not about 'love affairs.'"

Stendhal would have been scandalized, though also amused: Why not talk about love affairs? Aren't we interested in seeing how people relate to one another in all revealing situations? As a Frenchman, that was his way of dealing with the subject, and it issues into anecdotes that structure and embellish Stendhal's writing—to say nothing of Montaigne's, Saint-Simon's, Proust's, Sartre's, and so on. For Ortega the anecdotes and the love affairs are all irrelevant. He is a Spaniard; it is the *institution* of love that matters most to him.

The ability to love is central to human nature, just as hatred and selfishness are. In most of the twentieth century there was relatively little philosophy written about these aspects of reality. Ortega, too, is astounded by that hiatus in modern thinking. If the situation is ever remedied, his pioneering work will be appreciated. In this age of analysis, this age of techniques, this age of instrumental refinements, fuzzy subjects are left to fuzzy minds. There is no fuzzier subject than love; there are few minds less inclined to fuzziness than Ortega's. Here, as in his other work, his example can have a salutary effect on the barrenness of so much contemporary English and American philosophy. "Why write," he asks, "if this too easy activity of pushing a pen across paper is not given a certain bull-fighting risk and we do not approach dangerous, agile, and two-horned topics?"[16] That's the spirit. *¡Olé!*

9

Concluding Remarks: Love and Sex in the Twenty-First Century

In much of the twentieth century, people saw themselves as pioneers setting forth into a new world—and even a new humanity—that developments in technology would someday create. We who have now entered the next millennium tend to feel that we have already begun to live in the outer regions of that advanced condition. Though it is always hard to predict how human beings will change, we can possibly have some tentative ideas about the immediate future of love and sex.

Having discussed the morality of sex, love, and compassion in this book, and after arguing in its prequel that these three are internally related, I sense an evolution in each that may be occurring now. Throughout the idealizations of the nineteenth century, both sex and sexual love were often interpreted as directly produced by powerful organic forces in nature—what Kant would have referred to as impulsive "natural inclinations." These were thought to consist of the sensuous to some extent but mainly of the passionate in one or another manifestation. Young people felt justified in thwarting social and parental control of their mating behavior on the grounds that they were "madly" or even "desperately" in love. This attitude continues into the present, but as the twentieth century progressed each succeeding generation became more and more sophisticated about the perils of passion.

At specific periods, in the 1920s and even more so in the 1960s and 1970s, hesitancy about the passionate enabled the sensuous to flourish more than it had in the previous two hundred years. But, for the most part, sexual and even nonsexual love as normative states supremely worth attaining were still identified with the passionate. Harmful though it might sometimes be, passion was generally considered interpersonal sexuality at its best. Even in the later years of the twentieth century, romantic love—defined as fundamentally passionate—served as the most common ideal for erotic intimacy between men and women, and within a single gender.

Even so, passion does not have the appeal it once had. Being liberated, to whatever extent they are thus far, from preconceived assumptions about the innate capabilities of male and female, many people view their sexuality and desire for love in a fashion that differs greatly from the past. The invention of highly effective means of both contraception and extrasexual reproduction, as well as the increasing spread of the AIDS epidemic, has also deprived the passionate of its former glamor. It can no longer claim to be either the indubitable link to nature or the guarantee, when properly satisfied, of ultimate health and interpersonal happiness. As a rationale for sexual love before and after marriage, passion has lost the quasi-religious aura that once surrounded it. Yet people feel a need to love and be loved as they did in earlier centuries, although matchmaking may have become more difficult. The sensuous remains as an occasional, though highly attractive, solution for some men and women. But for most of them, it too is not sufficient by itself.

At this point the compassionate element and its associated feelings become more significant in the pursuit of love and sex. As I have been suggesting, compassion has ties with sympathy, empathy, identification, emotional oneness, friendliness, loving-kindness, and cognate means of uniting with other people and other animals. These affective realities deserve to be studied philosophically, above all in analytical philosophy, more thoroughly than they have been as yet. Regardless of how we finally distinguish them from each other, they all fall under the heading of compassion as that term is used in ordinary parlance. As a cluster of sentiments, they are akin to tenderness, sociability, benign concern, and general goodwill toward individuals with whom we wish to establish a physical bond. Therein lies their moral potentiality. But also they may be seen as revealing an instinct for gregariousness that affects the responses of human beings, who would otherwise feel estranged and alienated from any kindred spirit.

In the lifestyles of many couples nowadays, compassionate feelings may be replacing some of the ardor that passion creates. Compassion is not inherently cool, as the sensuous often is, but neither does it have the burning fervor that passionate need may ignite. At the same time, the three affective modes can be wholly compatible on any one occasion, though they vary in different circumstances and for different people. In the evolution of what it is to be a man or woman, we may be entering an epoch of increased acceptance of the interpersonal goods that the kindliness of compassion introduces into love and sex.

❋

When philosophers like Montaigne or Hume in the seventeenth and eighteenth centuries speculated about loving-kindness as a prime ingredient in a happy marriage, they were referring to its role in a sociable relationship that might be meager in both passion and the sensuous but wonderfully stable, satisfying, comfortable, familial, civilized, and pleasantly convivial. In its own moment of history, the twenty-first century may now be constructing a modern conception of love and sex that recognizes, more than nineteenth-century romanticism did, how valuable the compassionate mode can be whether or not, and to whatever degree, it is accompanied by either the passionate or the sensuous. This development may wreak havoc with what is known as falling in love, but not with the relationships that I have described as being in love and staying in love.[1]

The opinions of both Hume and Montaigne were more extreme than anything I believe. They overemphasized the differences between romantic love and married love. They thought that the companionate values that I mentioned were not needed in extramarital love affairs, and that sexual fulfillment or amorous excitement might well be an impediment in a good marriage. Separating the two kinds of intimacy in this way, these philosophers—like many other thinkers—denied that the contrasting attitudes can harmoniously coexist in feasible attachments. This is a doctrinal blunder that I have sought to rectify.

Since human sexuality is interpersonal as well as appetitive, and therefore contingent upon our entire spectrum of social feelings, the possible occurrence of compassion must be seen as internally related to sex on most or many occasions. There is nothing in the experience of romantic love, whether or not it is sexual, to exclude the benevolent and sociable sentiments that signify some compassionate response. Nor does the cordial and friendly concern that is fundamental in the ideal of married love preclude the continuance of sexual and romantic oneness between people who live together as spouses. On the contrary, the security and prolonged association that marriage legitimizes can increase the likelihood of consummations that are wholly sexual and romantic.

At times Hume and Montaigne seem to hold that even if a coalescence of the romantic and the marital might exist, they *ought* to be kept separate. This was the belief, fairly common at the time, that men should not treat their mistress and their wife as if they were alike. It is a view that has been exploded in the post-Freudian world we live in. We now realize that as far as sexuality and marriage are concerned, as well as the economic and political environments in which they occur, virtually all men and women may want access to the same or comparable types of relationship. Moreover, they want them as persons with equal rights and the autonomous capacity to make affective decisions on their own.

At this point we can return to our discussion of Kant and Schopenhauer. They disagree in the ways I pointed out: Kant could not perceive the potentiality for moral goodness in sexuality as distinct from married love, while Schopenhauer found marriage highly suspect except as a limited convenience. Nevertheless, the problems in their different theories arise from a similar inability on their part to comprehend that sex, love, and compassion interweave as related phenomena that may or may not be moral in a variety of social arrangements.

As we know, these arrangements are subject to historical transformations, both ideological and material, that reflect changes in human values as well as in the technology and types of economic production that interact responsively with those values. In our time the current synthesis that may give compassionate feelings greater importance in both sex and marriage might well be our species' way of coping with the altered circumstances in which it now finds itself.

While looking forward to that possibility, we can also benefit from the philosophies of Kant and Schopenhauer. In his own fashion, each of them presents views that pertain to our situation in the twenty-first century. They both saw very clearly that neither sex nor love nor the morality that these may embody can be reduced to passionate feeling alone. In that regard Kant is not at all a forerunner of Romantic ideology, though he is in other ways, and Schopenhauer is only a half-hearted representative of it.

✳

The present growth in population and relative affluence of the human race has had a vast and largely deleterious effect upon many animals with whom we share this planet. But in their personal affiliations among themselves, in their "love life," whatever it may be, members of animal species have not gone through the historical variability that humanity experiences from age to age. We are the only organisms that have a continuity of inherited ideas and ideals which not only manifests progressive alteration in affective responses but also contributes to the social mechanisms that cause many of the changes in this alteration. For that reason, perhaps, the patterns of love and sex within all other species have been remarkably uniform through time despite the massive interference by Homo sapiens. And though indigenous kinds of sensuous and passionate behavior are also cultivated by these animals, they do not operate in them as they normally do in us.

Animal passion is often very brief in its actual expression, and usually geared to the female's capacity for reproduction during ovulation. With the exception of a few nonhuman species, the sensuous—which is so pervasive throughout an animal's enjoyment of mere existence—belongs to its explicit sexuality mainly in the courtship phase. What seems most important for animals in relation to each other is their feeling that they are part of a kinship group with which they can identify themselves. The herd instinct is more evident with them than it is with us, and that may explain why animal males and females are so compliant in making themselves available for procreative purposes. The prolonged and promiscuous searching of the males, and the selective but finally submissive cooperation of the females— all this is enacted with a kind of selflessness that serves for them as something comparable to compassionate love in men and women.

I do not mean that animals might have the *same* kind of compassion or sympathy for one another as we do. They have little of our cognitive or imaginative aptitudes, which always mold and modulate the feelings of human beings. But also, in addition to acts of altruism and protectiveness toward those they care about, animals appear to be more happily at home within their immediate group than we are in ours. Despite their skirmishing for dominance and related privileges that come with rank, they have a placid acceptance of each other and their place in the social order which people find more difficult to achieve or even tolerate.

If I am right in thinking that the twenty-first century may be evolving new versions of sex and love that augment compassionate or quasi-compassionate feelings, we may be approximating the more selfless type of behavioral and affective bonding that most other animals have always had. This is not necessarily a good thing, but it is surely an engaging possibility, and worthy of further investigation.

Like all other developments in human nature, such prospects should be approached from the pluralistic point of view. That attempt to reorient our thinking about sex and love was one of the great advances in the second half of the twentieth century. By now the concept of a rainbow attitude toward sexual and amatory relations has received wider acceptance than ever before. Having surmounted the pre-Freudian ignorance of, and hostility toward, everything blatantly sexual, we are also outgrowing Freudian essentialism about the "normal" or the "natural" as predetermined categories. Just as we are amused by the quaintness of Benjamin Franklin's denigration of sexual intercourse because "the pleasure is brief and the position undignified," so too can we relish the Edwardian quip (whose implications were not fully appreciated when it was first uttered) that tells men and women "you can do whatever you want, as long as you don't do it in the street and frighten the horses."

The pluralist approach is inherently democratic, and its impact will be global now that the world is becoming more and more democratized. To all peoples alike pluralism extends a palette of differing colors from which each man or woman can make a choice at will without worrying about its innate rectitude. As a replacement for old rigidities about heterosexual or gay behavior, pluralism encourages the belief that these categories overlap and have both a variety of subdivisions that may be more, or less, suitable to any person, as determined for themselves by consenting adults.

The same is true of nonsexual love, which pluralism treats as an effort to accept, and to rejoice in, the endless diversity of beauty and goodness that every human being or other embodiment of life may possibly attain. Pluralism encourages us to foster that affirmative disposition. We have crossed this threshold only in recent years. It can lead us very far.

Notes

Preface

1. Irving Singer, *Feeling and Imagination: The Vibrant Flux of Our Existence* (Lanham, Md.: Rowman & Littlefield, 2001).
2. Irving Singer, *Sex: A Philosophical Primer* (Lanham, Md.: Rowman & Littlefield, 2001).

Chapter 1:
The Morality of Sex: Contra Kant

An earlier version of this chapter appeared in *Critical Horizons*, 1:2, 175–91.

1. Immanuel Kant, *Lectures on Ethics*, ed. Peter Heath and J. B. Schneewind, trans. Peter Heath (Cambridge: Cambridge University Press, 1997), 155–56.
2. Immanuel Kant, *Lectures on Ethics*, trans. Louis Infield (New York: Harper & Row, 1963), 163.
3. Kant, *Lectures on Ethics*, trans. Heath, 156.
4. For Diderot on *jouissance*, see my book *The Nature of Love: Courtly and Romantic* (Chicago: University of Chicago Press, 1984), 313–14.

5. David Hume, *A Treatise of Human Nature* (Oxford: Clarendon, 1888), 394.

6. Hume, *A Treatise of Human Nature*, 395.

7. On this, see Roger J. Sullivan, *Immanuel Kant's Moral Theory* (Cambridge: Cambridge University Press, 1989), 202.

8. Kant, *Lectures on Ethics*, trans. Infield, 167.

9. Kant, *Lectures on Ethics*, trans. Infield, 167.

10. See in particular *The Nature of Love: The Modern World* (Chicago: University of Chicago Press, 1987), passim; and *The Pursuit of Love* (Baltimore: Johns Hopkins University Press, 1994), 23–30.

11. On this development, see *The Nature of Love: Courtly and Romantic*, 376–431.

12. On Ficino's concept, see *The Nature of Love: Courtly and Romantic*, 174–75.

13. Friedrich Nietzsche, *The Gay Science*, trans. Walter Kaufmann (New York: Vintage, 1974), 319.

14. Bernard H. Baumrin, "Sexual Immorality Delineated," in *Philosophy and Sex*, ed. Robert Baker and Frederick Elliston (Buffalo: Prometheus, 1975), 116.

15. *Philosophy and Sex*, ed. Baker and Elliston, 122.

16. For further discussion of material in this chapter, see Alan Soble, *The Philosophy of Sex and Love* (St. Paul, Minn.: Paragon, 1998), 50–61; also his "Kant on Sex," included in program for 8 May 1999 meeting of Society for Philosophy of Sex and Love, together with reply by Natalie Brender entitled "Revisiting Kant on Sex." See also Allen W. Wood, *Kant's Ethical Thought* (Cambridge: Cambridge University Press, 1999), 256–82; Barbara Herman, "Could It Be Worth Thinking About Kant on Sex and Marriage?" in *A Mind of One's Own: Feminist Essays on Reason and Objectivity*, ed. Louise M. Antony and Charlotte Witt (Boulder, Colo.: Westview, 1993), 49–67; Christine M. Korsgaard, *Creating the Kingdom of Ends* (Cambridge: Cambridge University Press, 1996), 190–95; Rae Langton, "Love and Solipsism," in *Love Analyzed*, ed. Roger Lamb (Boulder, Colo.: Westview, 1997), particularly 126–40, also her companion essay "Sexual Solipsism," *Philosophical Topics*, 23:2; and Timothy J. Madigan, "The

Discarded Lemon: Kant, Prostitution and Respect for Persons," *Philosophy Now*, 21:14–16.

Chapter 2: The Morality of Compassion: Contra Kant and Schopenhauer

1. Immanuel Kant, *Grounding for the Metaphysics of Morals*, trans. Mary Gregor (Cambridge: Cambridge University Press, 1998), 38.

2. Kant, *Lectures on Ethics*, trans. Infield, 239–40.

3. Arthur Schopenhauer, *On the Basis of Morality*, trans. E. F. J. Payne (Indianapolis, Ind.: Bobbs-Merrill, 1965), 175.

4. Schopenhauer, *On the Basis of Morality*, 96. In this quotation from Kant, Schopenhauer italicizes the words *other human beings*.

5. Schopenhauer, *On the Basis of Morality*, 96.

6. Kant, *Lectures on Ethics*, trans. Infield, 240.

7. Immanuel Kant, *Grundlegung zur Metaphysik der Sitten* (Hamburg: Felix Meiner, 1962), 17.

8. Section 399, in Immanuel Kant, *Foundations of the Metaphysics of Morals*, trans. Lewis White Beck (Indianapolis, Ind.: Bobbs-Merrill, 1959), 16; Immanuel Kant, *Grounding for the Metaphysics of Morals*, trans. James W. Ellington (Indianapolis, Ind.: Hackett, 1981), 12; Immanuel Kant, *Groundwork of the Metaphysics of Morals*, trans. H. J. Paton (New York: Harper & Row, 1964), 67; Kant, *Grounding for the Metaphysics of Morals*, trans. Gregor, 13.

9. Kant, *Grounding for the Metaphysics of Morals*, trans. Ellington, 35, section 428.

10. Immanuel Kant, *Religion Within the Limits of Reason Alone*, 6:58/51. Quoted in J. B. Schneewind, "Autonomy, Obligation, and Virtue: An Overview of Kant's Moral Philosophy," in *Cambridge Companion to Kant*, ed. Paul Guyer (New York: Cambridge University Press, 1992), 328.

11. Immanuel Kant, *The Metaphysics of Morals*, trans. Mary Gregor (Cambridge: Cambridge University Press, 1996), 162.

12. Kant, *Metaphysics of Morals*, 201.

13. Kant, *Metaphysics of Morals*, 204.

14. Kant, *Metaphysics of Morals*, 205.

15. T. S. Eliot, *Murder in the Cathedral* (San Diego: Harcourt Brace Jovanovich, 1963), 44.

16. For discussion about Kant's critics, see J. B. Schneewind, "Autonomy, Obligation, and Virtue: An Overview of Kant's Moral Philosophy," in *Cambridge Companion to Kant*, ed. Guyer, 327–28; for references to some of Kant's critics, see 338–39.

17. Schopenhauer, *On the Basis of Morality*, 193.

18. Schopenhauer, *On the Basis of Morality*, 146.

19. Schopenhauer, *On the Basis of Morality*, 146.

20. Schopenhauer, *On the Basis of Morality*, 147.

21. Schopenhauer, *On the Basis of Morality*, 96.

22. Schopenhauer, *On the Basis of Morality*, 65. Words in italics omitted.

23. Schopenhauer, *On the Basis of Morality*, 210–11.

24. See my book *The Harmony of Nature and Spirit* (Baltimore: Johns Hopkins University Press, 1996), 184–87, 192–93. See also my discussion in chapter 7 of this book.

Chapter 3: Sexual Pluralism and Its Limits

This chapter is partly based on material, now revised, in my book *The Goals of Human Sexuality* (New York: Norton, 1973).

1. A. C. Kinsey et al., *Sexual Behavior in the Human Female* (Philadelphia: W. B. Saunders, 1953), 626.

2. Sigmund Freud, *General Theory of the Neuroses*, in *The Standard Edition of the Complete Psychological Works of Sigmund Freud* (London: Hogarth Press and the Institute of Psycho-Analysis, 1957 et. seq.), 16:328. Freud's complete works are hereafter referred to as *SE*.

3. See Alan Dixson, *Primate Sexuality: Comparative Studies of the Prosimians, Monkeys, Apes, and Human Beings* (Oxford: Clarendon, 1999).

4. Freud, *Civilization and Its Discontents*, in *SE*, 21:105.

5. Freud, "The Most Prevalent Form of Degradation in Erotic Life," in *Sexuality and the Psychology of Love* (New York: Collier, 1963), 68. Also, in a less preferable translation, in *SE*, 11:189.

6. Freud, *Sexuality and the Psychology of Love*, 69.

7. On this, see my book *The Pursuit of Love*, 125–43.

8. W. H. Masters and V. E. Johnson, *Human Sexual Response* (Boston: Little, Brown, 1966), 342.

9. Kinsey, *Sexual Behavior in the Human Female*, 639.

10. Kinsey, *Sexual Behavior in the Human Female*, 640.

11. Masters and Johnson, *Human Sexual Response*, 127.

12. Masters and Johnson, *Human Sexual Response*, 4.

13. Masters and Johnson, *Human Sexual Response*, 12.

14. Masters and Johnson, *Human Sexual Response*, 20, and 8.

15. Kinsey, *Sexual Behavior in the Human Female*, 638.

16. On this, see the glossary in H. Giese, *The Sexuality of Women* (London: Deutsch, 1970), 136.

17. On this, see my book *Sex: A Philosophical Primer*.

18. Mary Jane Sherfey, *The Nature and Evolution of Female Sexuality* (New York: Random House, 1972), 110.

19. Sherfey, *The Nature and Evolution of Female Sexuality*, 112–13.

20. Sigmund Freud, "'Civilized' Sexual Morality and Modern Nervous Illness," in *SE*, 9:177–204.

21. Quoted in Ernest Jones, *The Life and Work of Sigmund Freud* (London: Hogarth, 1958), 3:208–9.

22. For further analysis along these lines, see my book *Sex: A Philosophical Primer*, particularly 113–23.

Chapter 4: The History of Love

This chapter and the next one are partly revised versions of television interviews that were broadcast on TVOntario. Copyright © TVOntario. Reprinted with permission.

Chapter 6:
The Nature and Pursuit of Love Revisited

1. For further discussion of Nietzsche's concept of amor fati, see my book *Feeling and Imagination*, 175–78, 197–98, 206, 214n6.

Chapter 7: Sympathetic Intuition:
Henri Bergson

1. See George Santayana, "The Philosophy of M. Henri Bergson," in his *Winds of Doctrine* in *Winds of Doctrine and Platonism and the Spiritual Life* (Gloucester, Mass.: Peter Smith, 1971), 58–109. For Russell on Bergson, see notes 2 and 3 below.

2. Bertrand Russell, "Bergson," in his *A History of Western Philosophy* (New York: Simon and Schuster, 1945), 806.

3. Bertrand Russell, *Our Knowledge of the External World* (London: George Allen and Unwin, 1926), 155. For a fuller analysis, see Russell's chapter on "The Theory of Continuity" in *Our Knowledge of the External World*, 135–58. See also his pamphlet *The Philosophy of Bergson*, which also includes a reply by H. Wildon Carr and a rejoinder by Russell (Folcroft, Penn.: Folcroft Library Editions, 1971).

4. Henri Bergson, *An Introduction to Metaphysics*, trans. T. E. Hulme (Indianapolis, Ind.: Library of Liberal Arts, 1955), 24.

5. For Bergson on open and closed morality, see his *The Two Sources of Morality and Religion*, trans. R. Ashley Audra and Cloudesley Brereton, with the assistance of W. Horsfall Carter (Notre Dame, Ind.: Notre Dame University Press, 1977), particularly 18–39.

6. David Hume, *An Enquiry Concerning the Principles of Morals*, in his *Enquiries Concerning the Human Understanding and Concerning the Principles of Morals*, ed. L. A. Selby-Bigge (Oxford: Clarendon, 1902), 229.

7. On Bergson's philosophy in relation to Proust's, and in itself, see my book *The Nature of Love: The Modern World*, 162–70, 205–9, and passim.

8. For further discussion of Bergson's philosophy, see the following recent works: John Mullarkey, *Bergson and Philosophy* (Notre Dame, Ind.: Notre Dame University Press, 2000); *The New Bergson*, ed. John Mullarkey (Manchester, England: Manchester University Press, 1999); F. C. T. Moore, *Bergson: Thinking Backwards* (New York: Cambridge University Press, 1996); A. R. Lacey, *Bergson* (London: Routledge, 1989); and Gilles Deleuze, *Bergsonism*, trans. Hugh Tomlinson and Barbara Habberjam (New York: Zone, 1988).

Chapter 8: Ortega on Love

This chapter is a revised version of an essay that appeared in *The Hudson Review*, 11:1, 145–54.

1. José Ortega y Gasset, *On Love: Aspects of a Single Theme*, trans. Toby Talbot (New York: Meridian, 1957).

2. Ortega, *On Love*, 109.

3. Ortega, *On Love*, 20.

4. Ortega, *On Love*, 30.

5. Ortega, *On Love*, 12.

6. Ortega, *On Love*, 20.

7. Ortega, *On Love*, 41.

8. Ortega, *On Love*, 47.

9. Ortega, *On Love*, 19.

10. Ortega, *On Love*, 99.

11. Marcel Proust, *A la recherche du temps perdu*, ed. under the direction of Jean-Yves Tadié (Paris: Gallimard, 1987), 1:337. My translation.

12. Stendhal, *On Love*, trans. H. B. V. under the direction of C. K. Scott-Moncrieff (New York: Grosset and Dunlap, 1967), 6.

13. Ortega, *On Love*, 202.

14. Ortega, *On Love*, 188.

15. For a more highly nuanced discussion of Stendhal's ideas about love, see my book *The Nature of Love: Courtly and Romantic*, 351–75 and passim.

16. Ortega, *On Love*, 127.

Chapter 9: Concluding Remarks:
Love and Sex in the Twenty-First Century

1. On my distinction between falling in love, being in love, and staying in love, see my book *The Nature of Love: The Modern World*, 383–90.

Index

About the Author

Irving Singer is the author of many books, including *Sex: A Philosophical Primer; Feeling and Imagination: The Vibrant Flux of Our Existence; George Santayana, Literary Philosopher; Reality Transformed: Film as Meaning and Technique;* and his trilogies *Meaning in Life* and *The Nature of Love.* He is a professor of philosophy at the Massachusetts Institute of Technology.